CONTENTS

INTRODUCTION

When, now many years ago, I was involved in early research for the *Cronaca della Guerra del Vietnam* (*Chronology of the Vietnam War*) I ran across—I don't recall exactly where—references to some "Norwegians" who were engaged by the Americans in clandestine operations skippering fast motorboats along the North Vietnamese coast.

I didn't give much weight to the story, most of all because it seemed to me unlikely, but then, inside me, I thought, who knows what they meant to say, in reality, with "Norwegians" or "the Vikings"; a stranger in a strange land always runs the risk of being identified in a hasty or mistaken fashion, and such a nickname remains stuck to them forever.

Each war is a melting pot, and the war in Vietnam was more so than others. A single adventurer or mercenary can come from anywhere; we know of a Turkish pilot who served as a crew member with Air America, the airline controlled by the CIA for clandestine operations in Southeast Asia, as well as of a Japanese contractor (with twenty years' experience in the French Foreign Legion) who lost his life in Iraq in 2005. The fact, however, that a group of Norwegians, even though civilians, had been engaged by the CIA for operations in Vietnam, with the consent of the intelligence service of the Norwegian government, seemed to be truly unreal.

The news, however, was in itself too tantalizing to be written off without at least a superficial investigation. What I found out was that the deeper I dug, the more proof I found that this story was true. At first it seemed to be a treasure hunt, in which I always found myself at the starting point. All paths seemed to be dead-end streets or "cold trails." I read about a Swedish journalist by the name of Sven Öste who worked for *Dagens Nyheter*, who was supposed to have interviewed two of the Vikings. Unfortunately, Sven Öste had died in 1996; the people at *Dagens Nyheter* were very courteous when I contacted them, but were unable to find anything in their archives. They told me that in addition to working for *Dagens Nyheter*, Sven Öste had also worked as a freelance writer, so it was not a given that that interview had been done for them. In effect, Öste retired in 1990 but continued to work in his final years as a freelancer. With respect to my investigation, however, I was back to where I started from.

The turning point came when, some time later, I found out that the Norwegian NRK radio and television network had made a documentary on the subject, interviewing several of the protagonists. Through the good offices of the Norwegian embassy in Italy, I first contacted the director, Arild Aspøy, then the network directly. They were a bit surprised and suspicious because they could not understand what interest I could have in obtaining a copy of the DVD of that episode, which had been aired at such a late hour more than ten years earlier.

Meanwhile, I had begun to examine CIA files that had been declassified, in the volume *The Way We Do Things* by Thomas Ahern, in which the missions were reported with many details but without ever mentioning the name or the nationality of the "skippers," so that I could begin to put the pieces of the puzzle together.

In Rome, Cecilie Grina Iversen, who I will never be able to thank enough, who at the time was the assistant to the Norwegian military attaché in Italy, welcomed me to the embassy and translated "on the spot" the part the Norwegians played in the *Vi som støtter Amerika* ("We who support America") documentary. For the parts that were in English, there was no problem because all the Americans who had been interviewed spoke very clear English. There remained the parts in Vietnamese, and for that I enlisted my colleague and friend Văn Huyên Trường, who quickly translated the few parts that were spoken in his mother tongue.

At that point, the Vikings, as well as some of the Vietnamese and American personages who were involved in that far-off adventure, began to have a face and a story.

Wick Tourison, who had done research for the NRK in America both of the American and Vietnamese survivors, with a long telephone call and an intense exchange of emails, provided another essential contribution to my research.

Despite the time that had passed and the fact that some of the information had been made known, it is a story about which very little continues to be known, both in Norway as well as in the United States. The reasons are varied: in Norway, despite the decades that have passed, it seems to still be an embarrassment that even though publicly the Norwegian government was opposed to the American involvement in Vietnam, in reality it supported that involvement, with men as well as with equipment (the Nasty-class patrol boats). In addition to that, one of the three sailors continued, once they had repatriated, for personal or professional motives, neither the Norwegian military intelligence service nor any of the Norwegians involved had any reason to publicize the affair. In the United States, there are different reasons: above all, the "heroes" are not American, so the media lacked an interest in the story; in addition, this was an operation that by and large did not have a happy ending, so there were no triumphs to celebrate, not even after the passage of time. Finally, the South Vietnamese commandos had been sent into action without an official chain of command that could lead back to the United States, so they were set aside in postwar memory.

It is a pleasant surprise for me how much this story raised so much interest and how little other people know about it, even those who are into this type of subject.

As always, truth outdoes fiction.

PROLOGUE

Norwegian commanders leading patrol boats used to land commandos in North Vietnam. Today this might seem a contradiction in terms, or an unlikely urban legend. This little-known aspect of the war in Vietnam brings us back to the 1960s, specifically to 1963.

When the first fifty-four Vietnamese special-forces raiders, divided into three groups with their operating base at Đà Nẵng, were to be operationally employed (the story of the—most unfortunate—infiltrations via air with parachutes is another one, even though in some sense parallel), two problems arose at the same time.

The first was that the fast naval vessels needed for the planned coastal incursions were much more complex to skipper than junks and sampans with which they had operated up until then, and there were no personnel adequately prepared to command them. The second was the imperative to avoid those American nationals, even though acting as civilians or undercover, falling into the hands of the North Vietnamese, thus publicly demonstrating an active US involvement, which until that time had always been denied.

What led to contact with Norway and with these people?

The acquisition of special naval craft in Norway ("Nasty" boats) was an element that only coincidentally, but almost completely, coincided with the recruitment of personnel who had to be experts in navigation in coastal waters and not be of American nationality.

The CIA person responsible for clandestine naval operations, William "Bill" Hamilton (an officer coming from the US Navy, in which he had contributed to the creation of the SEALs, and who after his experience with the CIA reentered the navy), knew that the US Navy had acquired two patrol boats in Norway (the *Skrei* and the *Hvass* of the Tjeld class, known as "Nasty" boats) but did not have any specific missions to assign to these units. Hamilton then asked the navy if they could cede them to the CIA. The response was positive. [*Author*: In a later interview, Hamilton made specific reference to Adm. Arleigh Burke as the recipient of his request, but Burke left service as chief of naval operations in 1961, so it was not possible that it was he who in 1962 or 1963 was able to decide or deal with such a request, unless the undertaking had been discussed much earlier, at the time of the formation of the navy SEALs; Burke had in fact personally inspected the boat in May 1960 during an official visit to Norway. It is certain that he expressed interest in the *Tjeld* and that he had pressed for the acquisition of at least one of the first ships.] The fact that the boats were Norwegian-built made them suitable, at least for American intentions, to mask direct USA involvement in offensive missions against North Vietnamese territory. The minister of defense in Oslo and the Norwegian Westermoen shipyards, but not the rest of the Norwegian government, knew of the final destination of the boats (CIA, in Vietnam). That at least is one of the theories, more or less credible or founded, that circulated in Norway in that regard.

Independent of that acquisition, the problem had to be faced regarding recruitment of commanders to lead the American craft (Swift boats) used by the CIA for clandestine operations staging out of the base at Đà Nẵng. High-risk mission commanders for operations north of the seventeenth parallel, as mentioned, should not be Americans and had to be experts in navigating coastal waters.

Contacts in Norway had been set in motion on the initiative of the CIA station in Oslo, one of whose agents had excellent local contacts. The personnel who were recruited through a local maritime school, unquestionably with at least the tacit assent of the authorities (at least with the higher-ranking officers of the Norwegian intelligence service, if not directly with the government itself) were "the best people you could ever imagine," and as the facts proved, "they were superb" (Hamilton, interview in 2000). Moreover, physically "they looked like Americans" (Sedgwick Tourison, former US military intelligence officer and historian of clandestine operations in Vietnam, interviewed in 2000), which did not hurt, since it would make it easier for them to blend in with other Americans who were present as advisors and trainers in Vietnam, and given that they would also have American cover names.

The local "recruiter" was Alf Martens Meyer, a high-ranking officer in the Norwegian secret service and an emblematic figure in Oslo intelligence for several decades during the Cold War.[1]

The Americans, ever with an eye to having non-American personnel and limiting political risks and maintaining their image, through the CIA station in Bonn had also recruited five German sailors (a mechanic and four commanders) to captain *PTF-1* and *PTF-2*, former US Navy craft from the 1950s, called "Gassers" and returned to service for the occasion, and not the Swift boats, which were destined for the Norwegians. The failure in this case was total: the German sailors were often drunk (with a preference for cognac) and involved in party making in Đà Nẵng with prostitutes and all things added to and connected with that, with consequent problems with the South Vietnamese police. It also seems that in addition to not having the hoped-for competence, they treated the South Vietnamese allies (with whom they were supposed to operate) with condescension. For those reasons, as well as because of the risk that their behavior might compromise the secrecy of the program, their contract was canceled. In the end, the Americans repatriated them after barely a month in Vietnam, without them having completed a single mission. The Germans sought to stick to the contract, but with a lump-sum allowance, the Americans were able to unburden themselves with an amicable agreement. When, on April 26, 1964, the two "Gassers" returned from Subic Bay to Đà Nẵng, after repairs and improvements to the fuel tanks, the Germans had already been sent home.

In 1963, the Americans were still directly involved officially only to a small degree in Vietnam but were already, in an undercover way, engaged both on the political as well as the operational level with military advisors and CIA operatives and operatives of other agencies and parallel paramilitary entities. All of this was happening in Vietnam as well as in Laos.

In the context of clandestine operations contemplated by the Kennedy administration to exert growing pressure on North Vietnam, part of the plan was to land agents, commandos, and saboteurs on the North Vietnamese coast. The story that follows tells the tale of men who came to Vietnam, coming from another part of the world to command "under contract" naval craft engaged in high-risk missions in hostile waters along the North Vietnamese coastline. In addition, it tells of those South Vietnamese—or Americans, as they might be—who took part in the preparation and execution of those missions, often meeting, in the latter case, a tragic end.

Notes

1. Alf Martens Meyer, ex-captain of the Royal Norwegian Navy and during the war a member of the Milorg, the "secret army" of the Norwegian resistance, was the principal actor in Norwegian intelligence operations during the 1950s and 1960s. After retiring, during his final years Meyer moved to Spain. He is involved to some extent in all the stories, more or less romanticized, of espionage that involved Norway during the Cold War. Even allowing for the fact that Norway's human resources were necessarily limited from the numerical aspect, it seems that Meyer was to some extent the parsley needed by investigative journalists to give a flavor to any story that involved Norway and intelligence operations. Be that as it may, in this case his role in recruiting Norwegians is certain beyond all doubt. The fact that those currently responsible in the Norwegian defense establishment assert that Meyer, if he acted, acted privately and on his own initiative in the enlistment of Norwegians, does not lessen the credibility of the assertions by Tourison and Hamilton, who say that such an operation was substantially impossible by the Oslo CIA station without the consent of or at least information provided by high Norwegian government officials.

CHAPTER
1

Before the
Vikings

It is useful to review, with a brief chronological history, some of the principal clandestine operations and infiltration attempts, by air and by sea, of South Vietnamese commandos and intelligence agents to North Vietnam, beginning in 1961. Obviously, operations of the sort, or missions of shorter duration with insertion by foot across land borders, took place before, during, and after that period, but what is summarized in this chapter helps us frame the situation in the historical moment that we are looking at, prior to the arrival of the Norwegians in Vietnam. It also gives us an idea of the American strategy of applying a light but ever-increasing pressure on North Vietnam, with pawns that were considered "sacrificeable," with results that we shall see.

Excerpts from Alessandro Giorgi,
Chronology of the Vietnam War, 1961–1975

March 26, 1961. Infiltration by night landing, from a sampan, of a CIA informant in North Vietnam. The agent, who had already entered North Vietnam on the previous December 5 by crossing the Bến Hải River (Vietnamese: Sông Bến Hải) on a makeshift dinghy,[1] lands on the coast near Đồng Hới (in the southernmost North Vietnamese province of Quảng Bình). After four days he returns by land, crossing the Bến Hải. A subsequent infiltration in April by another agent (ARES) at Haiphong would end with the arrest, on June 17, of the agent and his brother, who had sheltered the infiltrated agent in his village of origin.[2]

May 27, 1961. Infiltration by airdrop from a C-47 piloted by future prime minister Major Cao Kỳ, of a group of four Vietnamese agents (Team Castor, sergeants of the South Vietnamese army originating from the province of Sơn La in the north), in a joint operation by the CIA and the PLO (Presidential Liaison Office, South Vietnamese intelligence agency under the command of Colonel Lê Quang Tung), in the district of Mộc Châu (province of Sơn La), in the northwest of North Vietnam. The aircraft is detected by North Vietnamese radar, and four days later the group is captured.

June 2, 1961. Infiltration by airdrop of another group of three informers (Team Echo) in a joint operation by CIA-PLO (yet unaware of the failure of the previous operation of May 27), in the southern part of North Vietnam

(Quảng Bình Province). The team manages to send only a single message, on June 23, when it already knew it had been spotted, before being captured by North Vietnamese security forces while attempting to cross the border with Laos.

June 29, 1961. Infiltration by airdrop of a third group of four informants (Team Dido) in a CIA-PLO operation, in the province of Lai Châu, northwest of the drop zone of Team "Echo." Within four weeks, before even having the chance to communicate with Saigon by radio, the group would be captured by the North Vietnamese.

August 3, 1961. In view of the ambiguity or total lack of messages from the groups of informants infiltrated in the north months earlier, the CIA headquarters at Langley are forced to accept the possibility that all the groups and the relative radio communications are actually in the hands of the enemy, and urge the Saigon station to reconsider the entire program. On August 1, the first "trial" had been held in Hanoi (Vietnamese: Hà Nội) of the crew of a plane shot down during a mission to drop supplies to the infiltration teams.

January 13–14, 1962. Failed attempt by CIA-PSO (Presidential Survey Office, the new name adopted by the PLO after the capture and trial of the C-47 crew on August 3, 1961) to bring supplies by junk (*Nautilus I*) to an agent infiltrated in the North on the islands in the northern approaches of the Gulf of Tonkin—the junk and crew are intercepted and captured by a North Vietnamese patrol boat. The infiltrated agent had in fact already been under North Vietnamese control since June 1961 (agent ARES, March 26, 1961). A further supply mission in mid-April, apparently successful, would encourage the Americans and South Vietnamese in the misguided belief that the infiltrator is free to act and fully operative.

February 20, 1962. Infiltration by airdrop from a Douglas DC-4 four-engine plane, piloted by Lt. Col. Cao Kỳ, of a team of five agents (Team Europe) into North Vietnam: within two days, the group would be captured by the North Vietnamese, who, using the captured radio, still intact, would attempt to carry out a disinformation operation (the mission had been authorized by the CIA on February 15, after discussions and misgivings regarding the methods, aims, and results of such missions).

March 12, 1962. CIA-PSO attempts to infiltrate a group of agents (Team Atlas) into North Vietnam: a helicopter transports the group (four Vietnamese volunteers) from Thailand to Laos near the North Vietnamese border, to be crossed on foot. Four days later the group is identified; in an attempt to escape, two of the members lose their lives, and on April 4 the survivors are captured and put on public trial.

April 16, 1962. A group of six agents (Team Remus, from the Thai mountain tribes known as the "Black Thai") are parachuted by the Americans onto the northern border between Laos and North Vietnam (15 kilometers northwest of Dien Bien Phu). The team would successfully operate in the agents' area of origin for two months before being identified and the members gradually being captured as of the following June 23.

May 17, 1962. A group of seven saboteurs (Team Tourbillon), transported by an aircraft with Taiwanese crew, parachutes into North Vietnam with the intention of joining the Castor group (the capture of which is at this time still unknown to the CIA and PSO from May 27, 1961). The North Vietnamese security forces, lying in wait in the launch area, kill one of the members and within two days capture the other six. Once again, the CIA and PSO fail to be alerted due to delays and inconsistencies in radio communications.

May 20, 1962. A group of five agents (Team Eros, composed of Hmong and "Red Thai" montagnards) are parachuted into North Vietnam in the province of Thanh Hóa, east of the northern border between North Vietnam and Laos. Here again, the commandos are quickly identified but manage to escape for several weeks. After a long "on again, off again" hunt on September 29, one member is killed and another captured by North Vietnamese security forces. The three survivors who arrive at the border are met by a group of Laotian hunters who, however, betray them and hand them over to the North Vietnamese.

June 28–30, 1962. A South Vietnamese junk from the CIA-PSO joint program [*Author: Nautilus III*. Tourison, in his *Secret Army, Secret War*, appendix 10, cites *Nautilus II*] transports a team of four South Vietnamese combat divers to the North Vietnamese naval base of Quảng Khê, at the mouth of the Gianh, 40 kilometers north of Đồng Hới, with the aim of sabotaging the naval units present (Swatow-class gunboats). The commandos' minelaying operations have already begun when the North Vietnamese units intercept and ram the junk. All the divers are killed, and the crew members are taken prisoner (except one, who hides on the drifting wreck and is rescued by the South Vietnamese the following day). A North Vietnamese motor gunboat is damaged. The insistence of US president Kennedy on attacks against the territory of North Vietnam has pushed the CIA station in Saigon to plan missions no matter what, using all available resources (Operation Vulcan).

August 23, 1962. The CIA deputy director (acting DCI), Lt. Gen. Marshall Carter, tells the assistant deputy director of plans (i.e., "clandestine operations"), Thomas Karamessines, that "the highest levels in the government [i.e., President Kennedy] have just approved a concept of intensified operations against North Vietnam." The aim is to "bring the war home" to the North Vietnamese and force Hanoi's leadership to "rethink" their strategy and military action and infiltration to the South.

December 24–30, 1962. A group of eight South Vietnamese saboteurs (Team Lyre) are infiltrated into North Vietnam by sea, carried by a junk. The operation was launched under the aegis of the SEPES (Service for Political and Social Studies; another cover name for another South Vietnamese intelligence and sabotage agency). In January, another team (Team Tarzan, six agents) would be parachuted, on the route through Laos, on road no. 12 in the southern part of North Vietnam.

April 13, 1963. A group of six South Vietnamese saboteurs (Team Pegasus, Vietnamese of Tho ethnicity, inhabitants of the mountainous regions of northern Vietnam, mainly Nghệ An Province, southwest of Hanoi) are parachuted 75 kilometers northeast of Hanoi, with the mission of sabotaging the railway linking Hanoi with China. Two weeks later, the first radio contact would be established with the Saigon CIA station: in reality, the group had already been identified and captured. In the following July, Hanoi would confirm the capture, which ended with a trial and long prison sentence.

May 14, 1963. Infiltration by parachute into North Vietnam of a group (Team Jason) of five saboteurs. This team is also quickly captured by the North Vietnamese security forces. In the following month of June, seven other groups of commandos would be parachuted into various areas of North Vietnam, all meeting the same fate. In the year of 1963 alone, thirty-four infiltrators from South Vietnam, entering by sea and by air, would be killed and 140 captured by the North Vietnamese.

May 29, 1963. Hanoi announces the capture of Team Lyre, the group of saboteurs that infiltrated on December 30, 1962.

July 2, 1963. In a joint CIA-SEPES operation, a group of raiders (Team Giant) are parachuted from a C-123 in the mountains west of the North Vietnamese city of Vinh (the south of the country). They would be followed on July 4 by another group (Team Packer), accompanied by two members sent to reinforce Team Europe (which had already been in the hands of the North Vietnamese for a year and a half, since February 15, 1962).

July 13, 1963. The South Vietnamese Team Dragon (six commandos of the ethnic Chinese Nung people) is infiltrated by junk (*Nautilus 7*) into Móng Cái, in the far north of North Vietnam, near the border with China, to sabotage an offshore radar station and contact suspected Nung dissidents in the area. The group is reported by local fishermen and immediately captured by North Vietnamese security forces.

August 28, 1963. Twenty-six Sino-nationalist commandos from Taiwan, after a stop on the Bạch Long Vĩ islet, land on the coast of the North Vietnamese province of Quảng Ninh, from where they intend to infiltrate the nearby Chinese border to form a nucleus of anti-Communist resistance. The North Vietnamese border guards, on alert after the South Vietnamese landing that took place only two weeks earlier in the same area (July 13; lack of coordination between Taipei and Saigon), immediately identify the group; seven commandos are killed in the gunfight, two commit suicide to avoid capture, and the remaining seventeen are captured and imprisoned.

August 11, 1963. Team Easy, made up of seven commandos of the Hmong and Thai ethnic groups, is parachuted by the CIA into North Vietnam, with a mission of subversion, intelligence, and sabotage.

September 4, 1963. The CIA-trained Team Swan is parachuted into the Cao Bằng area of North Vietnam with the combined mission of subversive propaganda, intelligence, and sabotage (similar to Team Easy, August 11). The group is almost immediately captured by the North Vietnamese.

October 27, 1963. In a joint CIA-PSO operation, an agent is infiltrated by sea north of Đồng Hới. The crews of the junk and dinghy in charge of the last phase of the approach return separately to South Vietnam, but the informant is not heard of again. The operation would be followed by two more raid attempts by sea against Quảng Khê's North Vietnamese naval base, both unsuccessful.

Notes

1. The agent in question, code-named "Hirondelle," was Vũ Công Hồng, a Catholic from the North who, at the last moment, told the Americans he could not swim, so he was hastily instructed to "paddle with both hands" as he was placed in the inner tube of a tire to cross the Bến Hải River. He was captured on his sixth mission, on September 17, 1961, while trying to infiltrate into the province of Nghệ An.

2. The agent in question, code-named "Ares," was Phạm Chuyên, a former member of the North Vietnamese Communist Party, originally from the northern province of Quảng Ninh, who fled to the South for personal reasons (his wife had left him for an army officer). After a difficult work of co-optation and a year of training, he was put ashore at the coal-trading port of Cẩm Phả, near Haiphong. When local fishermen, on April 9, accidentally came across the small boat he had come ashore in, the North Vietnamese authorities turned their suspicions to his family, with whom he had taken refuge, although he lived hidden in the forest. On June 11, his younger brother Phạm Do was arrested, followed on June 17 by Phạm Chuyên himself, who was then co-opted again by the North Vietnamese in an attempted disinformation operation against the Americans that lasted for years.

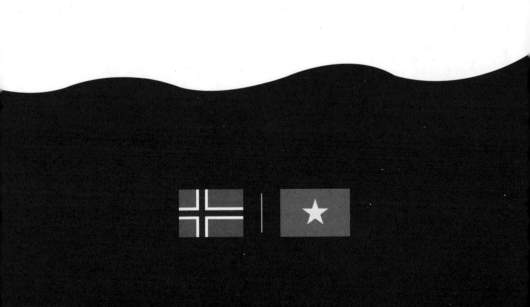

CHAPTER
2

First
Encounter

Bergen, on the southwest coast of Norway, July 1963, Hotel Bristol. Alf Martens Meyer, a high official in the Norwegian secret service (Etterretningstjenesten: E-tjenesten in the NIS = Norwegian Intelligence Service international designation), is about to meet, in one of the hotel's rooms, three sailors to propose a very particular job to them. It is not about going aboard a merchant vessel for a year or more, as was common among young Norwegians at the time. The three young men, Martin Vik, Knut Kalvenes, and Reidar Steffensen, still don't know it, since they also don't know who Alf Martens Meyer really is, but the contract that they are offered is out of the ordinary: on behalf of the CIA, to assume command of fast patrol boats in Vietnam, with the mission of landing South Vietnamese commandos and frogmen on the North Vietnamese coast for sabotage and reconnaissance missions.

All three had graduated with excellent references from the Bergen Sjømansskole, the nautical school in Bergen, one of the numerous Norwegian schools of that type. Knut and Reidar had graduated in 1962–63, while Martin had graduated from one of the immediately preceding classes. Martens Meyer himself was from Bergen, and many years earlier he had attended the same school and had then taught there, before and after the Second World War; he thus had contacts at the Sjømansskole who could recommend the best candidates. A few weeks later, they would board an aircraft headed to Saigon.

FLASHBACK: SCOUTING AND "THROWING THE BAIT"

In the spring of 1963, the young-but-already-experienced sailor Knut Kalvenes was contacted by an acquaintance from the maritime community in Austevoll (a municipality and archipelago on the southwestern coast of Norway, just south of Bergen), with a question about whether he might be interested in a mission as a maritime consultant in Asia. For the moment, not a word about Vietnam.

Knut was contacted because Alf Martens Meyer, who was closely connected to the shipping community in Bergen (and in Austevoll), had made a request among his acquaintances if they could think of any suitable guys for such a mission. Reidar, Knut, and Martin all had been sailing on the boats of Westfal-Larsen (Westfal-Larsen is a group of shipping companies, founded in 1918, and based in Bergen), and all three had attended the Bergen Seamen's School (Bergen Sjømansskole); Knut and Reidar in the same class, Martin a little earlier. Martin and Knut had sailed along the US West Coast at the beginning of the 1960s, then Knut disembarked to study at the Bergen Seamen's School, in Nordnes, where Reidar was taking the same class.

Martens Meyer, in addition to his good contacts, had also been teaching at Bergen Seamen's School for short periods before and after World War II. Whom Martens Meyer contacted in the first place, as intermediary and scout to get to the names of the three guys, is not 100 percent clear, but it may have been within the same circles: seamen, teachers, or former students at the school. Whether there had or had not been any contact with other candidates by Martens Meyer in the spring is unknown, but when Knut finally made up his mind about the mission, he was asked to find two colleagues who were equally skilled, trustworthy, and potentially interested.

Knut then contacted Reidar and Martin, and despite the vague information available, they all felt positive about the mission.[1]

Around mid-May, Knut, Reidar, and Martin received a formal letter, dated May 15, 1963, from a company in Panama, TASA Airlines, containing a more official proposal and request of their written confirmation, expressed by their signature for acceptance on the same latter, about their interest in the mission. The letter stated that the job was to work as "maritime advisor and instructor" in South Vietnam, and the contract was rather detailed for what concerned basic pay, benefits, insurance, and sick leave, but in vague terms as for the job description. It was made clear that TASA was acting on behalf of not-better-specified "maritime interests in South Vietnam," for which TASA was acting as a broker. It moreover stated that the final contract would be signed upon arrival in South Vietnam. The original paper shown in this book reports Knut's handwritten signature for acceptance, but we can assume that all three of them confirmed in the same way in their respective papers.

TASA, an "airline and general transportation company" based in Panama, was managed by an American couple, with local administration partners: the spouses were Michael D. Petrosky and his Italian American wife, Emilie Scarano Petrosky. TASA (Turismo Aéreo S.A.) had been established on February 9, 1954, in Panama, apparently only by Panamanian founding partners. On the contract proposal, besides the names of the two Americans, appears the name of a certain Arturo Müller Arosemena (elsewhere sometimes wrongly reported as "Miller"), qualified as president.

The names reported in the letterhead of the contract proposal in 1963 are, as already mentioned, Arturo Müller A. (A. for Arosemena, mother's family name), president, who figured within the founding members as treasurer back in the original board of 1954; Emilie S. Petrosky (née Scarano) as secretary; and Michael D. Petrosky himself, executive vice president and treasurer. After their marriage in April 1941, Michael and Emilie lived in Maryland, United States, then in Germany (possibly with Michael as member of some Allied occupation force, or intelligence, but that's just my speculation), and then moving to Panama, where they "owned and managed" TASA Airlines. Michael died in 1980. Some time after Michael's death, Emilie, after forty years in Panama, moved back to Ft. Lauderdale, Florida, and then to North Carolina, where she originally resided. Emilie Scarano Petrosky died, aged ninety-six, on October 28, 2015, in Mitchell County, North Carolina. There is a certain Michael Petrosky who at present is senior vice president of Air Panama, likely the son of Michael (Sr.) and Emilie: as a matter of fact, in Emilie's obituary it is quoted that Michael Petrosky is their son.

BACK TO THE BRISTOL HOTEL IN JULY

Before the meeting, the three young sailors were unfamiliar with the man they were supposed to meet, but they knew of course that it was all about the job they had been offered for South Vietnam. The meeting would take place in mid-July. At the reception, they were greeted by Alf Martens Meyer, and they then followed him up to the hotel room Martens Meyer had rented, so that they could talk undisturbed. Over a cup of coffee, they got a few more details about the mission, but apart from the fact that it was about maritime advice for the South Vietnamese navy and about being the master of small high-speed vessels, few details were yet given about who the hiring company (CIA) really was and what kind of mission it was going to be. They would travel via London to South Vietnam.

The proposal called for a compensation of $10,000 annually (although it specified that the period of service was to begin upon actual arrival in Vietnam), which for the times was a decidedly high salary even by American standards, plus holiday periods, complete coverage of moving expenses, food, lodging, and insurance coverage in case of death.

Meyer accordingly engaged Martin, Knut, and Reidar with an annual contract. When the meeting at the Hotel Bristol took place, as said, the three men—in addition to not knowing that Meyer was one of the most powerful men in Norwegian military intelligence—had no idea that the subject of the meeting and the proposal would in reality be wartime service in Vietnam, but, however, they did not hesitate to accept. The motives for their agreement were not strongly influenced by ideological positions: they were basically pro-American, but nothing more than that. It should also be taken into consideration that at the time, for young and very young Norwegians, getting on a boat and going to sea for long periods to "get to know the world" was quite a common step in the journey of formation and personal growth. Knut says: "We didn't think too much about it [before accepting]."

Notes

1. In an interview in 2020, Reidar said that he had a meeting with Martens Meyer together with an American in a hotel room at Hotel Neptun (in Bergen) in the spring of 1963, but in a later conversation with Jan Tore Nilsen toward the end of 2020, he was unsure about this meeting.

CHAPTER 3

Here Come the Vikings

SETTLEMENT IN ĐÀ NẴNG

August 1963: Arrival at Đà Nẵng

At the beginning of August, Knut, Reidar, and Martin traveled together to London. They spent a few days in London, where they had a new meeting with Martens Meyer and an American. This was probably the first time they got some more details about the mission, and it became very clear that it was in fact the Americans they would work for while they were in South Vietnam. From London, the three guys continued to Saigon, via Bombay (today Mumbai, India). A long journey, on civilian propeller planes.

In mid-August, Knut, Reidar, and Martin arrived in Saigon. Shortly after arrival, on August 15, they were taken to a meeting at the headquarters of the South Vietnamese navy in Saigon. In this meeting, they met for the first time their new official clients, the South Vietnamese CSF (Coastal Security Forces; not yet CSS, Coastal Security Service, to be established officially as such the next April), as well as a couple of Americans also attending the meeting. According to Reidar, this was the first time it was completely clear to him that the real client was the CIA. At the meeting, they finally signed the contracts for the mission, where the conditions they had previously accepted in the letter from TASA Airlines were confirmed. The contracts, drafted in English and Vietnamese, were signed by two South Vietnamese officers as representatives of the authorities, as well as by Knut, Reidar, and Martin. Reidar's contract shows that it was witnessed by Knut (we can assume they witnessed for each other) and signed by two officers from the South Vietnamese CSF. The contract states the following about the obligations the mission entailed: "The contractor will act as a maritime advisor to the Coastal Security Forces (CSF) of the government; act as a Master of a CSF patrol craft performing duties normally expected of a licensed Merchant Marine Master and, if required, perform combat duties of a Navy Ship Captain. Additionally, the contractor will supervise the training of his crew in naval matters pertaining to the operational missions of his craft."

The contract also contained, among other things, details about salary and compensation, as well as a compensation scheme if they should lose their lives during the mission or be taken prisoner. According to the contract, in addition to the salary of $10,000 US for the whole year term, there was a bonus for each completed mission. In addition, they had travel, clothing, food, and lodging covered. The contract was for one year but could be terminated before expiration with a thirty-days notice. It is further written that it would be terminated without notice with no further compensation if relatives showed up in the operating area.

The three Norwegians were given by the CIA, with little imagination, the cover name of the Vikings. In Saigon, they were told that they had to wait until everything was ready in Đà Nẵng, the port city, not far from the border with North Vietnam, which the Americans had chosen as the main base for secret naval operations against North Vietnam.

While they were waiting, they had already changed their identities. From then on, they would be called Pete (Knut), Mike (Martin), and Dick (Reidar). A surname would not be necessary and in fact was to be avoided.

In August 1963, Saigon was still a city with relatively few strangers. It was a bubbly and warm city with a lively population, but with a corrupt regime that was already struggling to survive both internal and external enemies. Society in South Vietnam was infiltrated by agents from Communist North Vietnam and was so corrupt that only strong American support kept it on its feet.

In Saigon there was the curfew, and they were equipped with an ID card from the authorities so that they could move through Saigon more safely if they were stopped by a patrol. The three guys stayed in Saigon for about a week, before boarding a smaller plane that took them north to Đà Nẵng.

Knut Kalvenes was born on September 14, 1936; therefore, in summer 1963 he was twenty-six years old, and about to turn twenty-seven in September. Reidar Steffensen was twenty-five, born in 1938. Martin Vik, the eldest, was born in 1935, so in 1963 he was between twenty-seven and twenty-eight.

In Saigon the CIA's Combined Studies Group (CSG) was managing both the air and sea infiltration program from a facility separate from the US embassy. Col. Gilbert Layton, CSG chief, procured aircraft and boats, with the main airbase at Tan Son Nhut and the forward boat base at Đà Nẵng. Col. Layton delegated control of the boat base to Tucker Gougelmann, a legendary figure in CIA clandestine operations.

August–November 1963: Training, Buildup, and Preparation

Around August 22 or 23, Knut, Martin, and Reidar (alias Pete, Mike, and Dick) arrived in Đà Nẵng. They were installed in a mansion, a big villa in one of the best neighborhoods in Đà Nẵng, where they had all they needed. In the house, they had a gardener, a cook, and a maid, and all expenses were covered by the CIA.

These operations were controlled by the CIA, and one of its essential elements, as with most other secret operations, was that no one should be able to connect US intelligence or authorities regarding what happened.

One can wonder if Norwegian intelligence and the Norwegian authorities would have been able to do the same, but given that the three sailors had been taken on as civilian contractors, the authorities in Oslo also could always have been able to say that they were in the dark about it.

The operational naval base was on the point of the Đà Nẵng Peninsula, at the base of the so-called Monkey Mountain.

The first months in Đà Nẵng were spent in training along with the South Vietnamese naval raiders. They trained in navigation, which at the time was based on the stars and compasses, and in infiltration of North Vietnam. The physical/athletic and technical/tactical training of the Vietnamese commandos was taught separately by SEAL instructors (Detachment ECHO of SEAL Team One) and American Marines.

RAdm. (ret.) Cathal "Irish" Flynn, at the time one of the instructors in Đà Nẵng (as a young platoon officer, UDT Eleven and SEAL Team One, and later as a SEAL detachment commander with Studies and Observations Group [SOG], Vietnam), declared in a later interview that back then, he found that young, freshly graduated American officers coming from the United States were very arrogant while teaching and lecturing veteran South Vietnamese soldiers; many of these South Vietnamese commandos had already been through combat in active service.

The working day often started with gymnastics and training. Reidar says that he often started the day with light physical training with the crew on the pier; movement, push-ups, and sit-ups. Martin says that one of the guys from the US Navy SEALS wanted him to join them in the "bush" for running and training with the special forces. This quickly ended when Martin reminded him that his contract was to command a boat, and not running around in the woods.

Normally, they walked or took a bicycle taxi from their house to the quay, where they were picked up to be driven out to the base. They were taken out to the base in a smaller boat, manned by Vietnamese. The trip out went along a pier, just west of the city. Reidar sometimes had migraine headaches, and Martin remembers one morning when Reidar could not get out of bed because of this. In the end, they just had to get down to the shuttle boat, without Reidar. Shortly afterward, however, Reidar could eventually get up, and luckily he managed to hitchhike with some Americans who were going out to the base.

The three soon earned the respect both of the South Vietnamese as well as the Americans. The then captain Trương Duy Tài, commander of the South Vietnamese Sea Commandos ("Lực Lượng Biệt Hải," or, in short, "Biệt Hải"), who later reached the rank of lieutenant colonel and after the war managed to escape to the United States and settle in New Orleans, Louisiana, remembers them thus: "They were *real* Vikings. They knew about navigation so well" (Dale Andradé, in *Conboy and Andradém*, 2000.).

Frogman Vũ Đức Gương, interviewed in 1989 by Wick Tourison, recounts the first training mission in November 1963, an exercise against the South Vietnamese navy base at the mouth of the Cửa Việt, a river just south of the Demilitarized Zone (border between the two Vietnams), but the winds were too strong, and their boats were unable to land.

Captain Trương Duy Tài, with his thirty-six commandos divided into six squads, reported to Major Ngô Thế Linh, commander of the Coastal Security Service (CSS, successor to the CSF from April 1964 onward), of which the Biệt Hải were the shock force.

At Đà Nẵng, the CIA person in charge and coordinator for naval operations was Tucker Gougelmann, a picturesque as well as legendary personality in CIA clandestine operations.

Gougelmann had been sent to Vietnam in 1962, where, after an initial assignment to the paramilitary training center at Hòa Cầm, near Đà Nẵng, he had requested and was put in charge of the (then still embryonic) clandestine naval operations, in conjunction with the PSO (Presidential Survey Office), the previously mentioned intelligence activity cell in South Vietnam, under Colonel Lê Quang Tung, chief of special forces and a faithful follower of President Diệm.[1]

Gougelmann, a former Marine colonel from the Second World War, after having left the Corps had joined the CIA, with which he had gained experience in special operations during the Korean War (infiltrations along the North Korean coast). It seems that he was also involved in the attempted anti-Castro invasion of the Bay of Pigs in Cuba in July 1961.[2]

In 1963, assisting him in Đà Nẵng was a young officer from the then newly constituted Navy SEALs, specifically from SEAL Team One, Lt. j.g. Phil Holtz. In the CIA, Holtz held increasingly important positions, until he became chief of station in San José, Costa Rica, at the time of the Iran-Contra scandal in Nicaragua, an affair in which he was directly involved.

Even after 1964, as we shall see later, when clandestine naval operations were transferred to MACV-SOG military officers, in reality those officers continued to be forced to avail themselves of the irreplaceable operational experience of the CIA group until autumn of 1964.

Shortly after arrival, they were introduced to the Swift boats on which they would operate. The choice of the American-made Swifts was apparently contradictory in terms of "plausible deniability," but it was considered acceptable as an interim solution. The vessels, made by Sewart Seacraft in Berwick, Louisiana, were bought by the CIA and, after modifications and testing in 1962, shipped by rail to San Diego, California, for further trials in spring 1963. Three of them were shipped (deck-loaded) to Subic Bay, Philippines, then ferried to Saigon, from where they had been sailed to Đà Nẵng by the Americans. Phil Holtz was among the guys sailing them up north. When the Norwegians arrived, only two of the three vessels were moored in Đà Nẵng; the third and last Swift arrived about a week later. One of the boats was a bit "overgrown," so it was docked on an island just outside the base, cleaned, and repainted.

The Norwegians had had no previous experience with this type of boat, nor had they been given any specific previous training in its use. They had what they described as an "on-the-job training." None of them considered this a special challenge, since they all were used to sailboats from an early age. Apart from the fact that the boats were a little faster than they were used to, they saw no difficulty. They found the Swift boats easy to operate, fast, and very maneuverable, with engines and levers that were easy to handle. US personnel took care of the maintenance on the machinery and ensured that the vessels were ready for sailing. The Norwegians were also given a four-page operating manual for what was called "Standard Operation Plan for a Maritime Exercise."

On Reidar's training-activity schedule for May 11–16, 1964, the type-written daily planned activity for the week for each of the three Vikings, with time indication (e.g., 0800–1200 for the morning, 1400–1700 for the afternoon), can be read, identified by and associated with the respective

Swift numbers (from top to bottom) 1, 2, and 3. For example, "Language class," "Exercise. Area to be determined," "Fuel," "Vega" (referring to the commando team VEGA), "Gen. Drills," "Site 4 ETA 2330," "RB [rubber boat?] Vectoring," etc. Plus, some scribbled notes, handwritten probably by the Vikings themselves. The days with activity are Monday through Friday, implicitly confirming that weekends were usually free. Although a document dated very late in time during their term, just before their last operative mission, it gives the basic idea of the working days' routine.

In the beginning the boats were not equipped with a radar. They had it fitted sometime after the first of the year in 1964, after they themselves had asked to have it. However, they were instructed not to use the radar during the missions, to reduce the risk of being detected and intercepted. Martin said he never used radar while on a real mission, while Reidar said he used it sometimes to facilitate navigation toward the drop point.

Knut Kalvenes, with his accent of the fjords of the south-central Norwegian coast, recounted thirty-six years later: "The South Vietnamese performed sabotage and reconnaissance missions. They always acted at night. Sailing up north it was cold, but I was always concentrating on the mission."

A radio direction (or detection) finder antenna was also fitted to the vessels. With this device, they could find direction, and the signal power was helpful to judge the distance. In addition, much of the sailing was based on sextant and compass and manual mechanical tools, and they were equipped with nautical charts that were not always of top quality. On board they also had night-vision goggles (infrared). With these they could see the infrared light signals from a "metascope" that the swimmers and the rubber inflatable boat were equipped with. This made it easier to spot the swimmers returning at the end of the mission. In addition, the Swift had a sort of infrared "head-light" on the helmsman's house that could not be seen with the "naked eye" but that could be seen by the swimmers, who also had infrared binoculars. They could also communicate with the men in the dinghy via radio, but this was to be avoided unless strictly necessary.

The vessels were equipped with light weapons. Behind the bridge roof, there was one .50-caliber (12.7 mm) machine gun. This was initially mounted on a temporary installment but was later mounted more properly in a permanent mounting. The vessels did not have a log speedometer, so speed was estimated on the basis of engine rpm and personal experience. No written logbook was kept on board, but the captain was equipped with a tape recorder on which rudder orders, change of course, and the like were recorded. The tape recorder was handed over to the Americans upon arrival at the base. The vessels were further equipped with VHF and HF radios.

Highly qualified mariners such as the Norwegians and the South Vietnamese raiders together in theory constituted a powerful weapon. Reidar and Knut had words full of praise for the South Vietnamese raiders and frogmen: "We found them to be brave and sympathetic, even though some of the frogmen were a bit crazy."

October 12, 1963: Leave and Wedding for Reidar

A few days before October 12, Reidar was granted a leave, and permission to travel a few days to Norway. Reidar and his fiancée, Liv, had decided to get married (she was pregnant), and the wedding was planned for October 12. They then traveled a few days to Paris on their honeymoon before Reidar traveled directly back to Đà Nẵng and Liv traveled back to Norway.

ASSASSINATIONS

On November 1, 1963, President Diệm was ousted from power by a coup d'état and later assassinated along with his brother Nhu, head of the secret services. The coup had been ordered by several South Vietnamese generals. In reality, the United States had given a decisive impulse to and approval of the coup, despite the fact that there had been much division and disagreement within the CIA and between the CIA and the State Department.

On November 22, 1963, President Kennedy was killed in Dallas. In the period immediately following the assassination, conditions in Đà Nẵng were chaotic, and "Pete," "Mike," and "Dick" were confined to their quarters while the Americans sought to understand how the situation was going to develop and find out what had happened. Given that on November 1, Diệm had been overthrown, in South Vietnam the situation was far from peaceful and clear. When their house arrest was lifted, they were told that the Americans would take them under their protection in case it was necessary to evacuate Đà Nẵng.

One of the consequences of Kennedy's assassination was that the newly installed President Lyndon Johnson ordered a further escalation of clandestine operations in the wake of the policy that Kennedy had put in motion. On January 16, he signed National Security Action Memorandum 273, which had been issued the previous November 26 (cf. "Chronology" in appendix 1), and the result of that order was a series of operations under the code name 34 Alpha or OPLAN 34A (which also included under that designation the actions of the Norwegians from February 1 onward).

Notes

1. Lê Quang Tung would be assassinated on November 1, 1963, by the coup members who on that same date had overthrown Diệm and then tracked him down and killed him the following day.

2. Gougelmann (the birth and death dates shown on his Arlington National Cemetery tombstone are January 24, 1917–June 23, 1975, but the latter is just the last day he was seen alive) was a US Marine Corps colonel, World War II veteran, and a CIA officer in their Special Activities Division. During the war, he served in the Pacific. During the Solomon Islands campaign, he suffered a severe wound in the right leg. Although the military doctors told him that his leg would have to be amputated as part of his treatment, Gougelmann was intent on returning to service and therefore refused to give his permission for the doctors to proceed with the amputation. He wound up keeping his leg, but as a result his convalescence lasted for two years. A former CIA officer who has worked with him told the author that "Tucker was a very close friend; I worked with him many times. It always amazed me how well he could function with the loss of a leg." Gougelmann remained in the Corps until his honorable discharge in 1949, then joined the nascent Central Intelligence Agency.

Gougelmann's first assignment was to Korea during the Korean War from 1950 to 1953, for covert operations, including helping agents to infiltrate the North. His experience was subsequently put to use by the CIA in the mid-1950s to the early 1960s in Cuba, Afghanistan, Europe, Tibet, and Vietnam. He used to wear a Tibetan ring that he maintained was taken from the finger of a dead Tibetan monk ("I cut it off the hand of a dead Buddhist monk," he said, grinning), but it was never ascertained if that was just a story to impress the interlocutors. It could be either way.

In 1962, Gougelmann was assigned to South Vietnam. He continued to specialize in covert operations, coordinating the Swift boat raids covered in this book, among other things. Following the takeover by the military, Gougelmann was assigned to the CIA's Saigon Station for domestic counterintelligence work with a local governmental entity. Gougelmann began a family life there with a local woman.

Gougelmann retired from the CIA in 1972, and before the fall of Saigon was living in Bangkok, Thailand, as a civilian. When his family could not be evacuated from Saigon prior to the impending North Vietnamese victory, he returned on his own. He reestablished contact with his family but couldn't get them out of the country. In the environment of that time, his presence was obviously very unsafe, to say the least.

Although he tried his best to hide, he was eventually found by the police on the advice of a local Vietnamese, after the fall of Saigon in April 1975.

Gougelmann was immediately arrested and kept in the main prison of the area, Chí Hòa Prison. A French reporter had witnessed his arrest, and he was reportedly seen by Vietnamese prisoners in Wing ED, where he was being kept. The Vietnamese government denied that they were holding him, despite being presented with evidence to the contrary. Details of his imprisonment are limited and unconfirmed (as the possible presence of Soviet intelligence officers during his interrogations), and his treatment by the Vietnamese during his captivity is based on examination of the evidence after the fact.

The Vietnamese government continued to deny that they were holding Gougelmann for the remainder of 1975 and 1976, but in 1977 they released his remains to US authorities. Postmortem examination by US government officials indicated that Gougelmann was tortured during his captivity, as evidenced primarily by a very large number of broken bones that appeared to have been broken and rebroken after healing.

According to CIA spymaster Orrin DeForest in his book *Slow Burn: The Rise and Bitter Fall of American Intelligence in Vietnam*, the story is totally different: Gougelmann had been retired and living in Saigon since 1973 with his Vietnamese wife. DeForest stated: "He could have gotten out easily enough, but he was a hard-nosed son of a bitch and he decided not to. He considered himself, practically speaking, a Vietnamese citizen. And he was not the kind of guy who would back down from anybody. He was retired, he told me when I last saw him, completely separated from any government work. Why should he get out for these pissants? He'd be damned if he was going to let anyone drive him away. Tucker was a stubborn man, tall, strong, and in excellent health. He was not the kind to die of malnutrition, not in the six months Hanoi had him before they shipped his body back home. I knew in my heart that they had tortured him to death."

According to yet another source (Douglas Valentine, *The Phoenix Program* [New York: William Morrow, 1990], 417–18), knowing that the country was doomed, Tucker Gougelmann wrote a letter to a friend on April 13, 1975, spelling out his plans to rescue his family. Posted from Bangkok, where he managed Associated Consultants Limited, Gougelmann's letter told how he planned his "extraction from Phu Quoc Island to Trat near Chantaburi on the southernmost part of the Thai east coast." Gougelmann commented on the "totally undependable" ARVN and its "cruel perpetrations on civilian refugees" and noted that "[Van] Thieu has killed SVN [South Vietnam]." He closed the letter with "C'est la fucking vie."

Before leaving Bangkok for Vietnam, Gougelmann asked a friend to try to get his family, including his youngest son, Edward, who was born after Gougelmann's arrest, out of Vietnam and to America if he ran afoul of the Vietnamese authorities. After contacting American government officials in the CIA and Congress, the friend succeeded in obtaining visas that allowed the family to immigrate to the United States.

After Gougelmann's remains were returned to the United States, he was buried at Arlington National Cemetery. His grave is located next to that of Francis Gary Powers.

Though he was not serving in an official capacity at the time of his arrest in 1975, the CIA decided that Gougelmann's death was a result of the official CIA activity that he had been involved with previously in Vietnam, and granted him a black star on the CIA Memorial Wall at CIA Headquarters in Langley.

CHAPTER 4

The Missions

Martin, Knut, and Reidar were each assigned to their own permanent Swift, which was not marked with a pennant number and didn't have any flag but was still given the number 1, 2, or 3. Knut had boat no. 1, Reidar no. 2, and Martin no. 3. A permanent crew of three South Vietnamese were attached to each of the boats: a helmsman, a machine gunner, and an interpreter / liaison officer. The crew members lived not far from the base. The Norwegians took a course to learn Vietnamese, first and foremost, in order to be able to give orders, especially rudder orders, on board in Vietnamese. Knut was the one who was best at Vietnamese, not least because his tone of voice was allegedly well suited for this language.

The briefs were usually held in the White Elephant Building. The building, located in 52 Bạch Đằng Street, was built by the French as a hotel, but in 1963 it housed both the South Vietnamese command as well as the American MAROPS command, later to become the so-called US Naval Support Activity, which included what was later to officially become the NAD (Naval Advisory Detachment) from February 1964. This was, among other things, the place where the chief of such operations, Tucker Gougelmann, lived at the time.

When new operations were planned, training and exercises were carried out in the area around Đà Nẵng before implementation. One of the favorite theaters for such exercises was the South Vietnamese naval base at the estuary of the Cửa Việt River, where they could simulate attacks against similar North Vietnamese naval bases located at the mouth of the rivers Gianh and Ròn up north.

The day before the action, the skipper tasked for the mission was briefed at the White Elephant. Only the skipper who was to perform the mission took part in the briefing, usually with two Americans. If there were two simultaneous missions, the two captains were briefed individually and kept separate. There was no one else present, normally. After the briefing, they had to stay and spend the night in the building where the briefing had taken place, until they were transported down to the quay to start the missions. They were not allowed to communicate with anyone else until the mission was completed. Basically, the briefings were often quite simple, including some information about possible threats, time of departure, how many men and from which team they would have on board, and which position they should go to. Most often, understandably, the missions were planned for moonless or nearly moonless nights. Martin says that sometimes the briefs were too simple and undetailed.

The teams of the South Vietnamese commandos were kept separate before the missions, and they were briefed in a different place than where Knut, Reidar, or Martin was briefed; the Norwegians did not take part in these briefings. The South Vietnamese were briefed by officers from the US Navy SEAL team and would go into details on the plan of the actual attacks on land or underwater. Missions could also be reconnaissance and intelligence, and preparation might include the preemptive study of images taken from satellites or airplanes. The members of each team designated for the mission also had to stay together, with each team separate from one another, and were not to leave the base until they were transported to the quay for boarding. This was for security and secrecy: to prevent leaks and to make sure they would not know more than they needed if someone was to be captured. These measures did not prevent, as we will see, leaks and compromission of the operations.

The Norwegians wore unmarked khaki uniforms. They all had their Colt .45 as a personal weapon, and in addition they occasionally trained with submachine guns. Reidar is portrayed with an M3A1 "Grease Gun" with the flash suppressor, similar to the type issued to the South Vietnamese commandos, which normally had an integral sound suppressor instead. Other common submachine guns in the theater for "unofficial" usage were the Swedish Carl Gustaf M/45B or the French MAT-49, or North Vietnamese adaptations of Soviet or French weapons. The Norwegians brought their pistols home with them, just in case of need. They mostly felt safe, but you could never quite know. The South Vietnamese on board did not have rank insignia either. The team that was to complete the missions on land was normally below deck during the voyage up to the target. On the aft deck, there were typically one or two rubber inflatable boats, ready to be put to sea. In addition, the Swifts were equipped with a larger rubber tank full of extra fuel. This was secured on the deck and sometimes proved necessary, to make it back to Đà Nẵng.

The operation, as said, was usually briefed the day before, and the very day of the action the captains were driven (or walked or took a bicycle taxi) down to the quay and picked up in a small boat for transport to the operational base where the Swifts were stationed, maintained, and refueled.

From the Swift base, they went to a pier in another part of the city, where they took the raiders aboard. While the Americans in charge of the operation remained on the pier, the Vietnamese and Norwegians headed north. Along with the Norwegians aboard the Swift boats were at least a dozen Vietnamese: minimally four members of the assault team, plus one or two members tasked with surveillance or handling the rubber raft awaiting the return of the raiders. The other three on board were, as previously specified, the helmsman, the interpreter, and the machine gunner for the .50-caliber machine gun. The aluminum hull with very shallow draft and two Detroit Marine Diesel engines gave it a maximum speed of 28 knots, a novelty for the Norwegians, who had never skippered such fast boats.

The missions always left in the afternoon, with eight to ten hours of navigation to penetrate deep into enemy waters.

They normally passed the seventeenth parallel under the cover of darkness. Typically they would sail out to the open sea and then continue north. If there were two Swifts on the mission, they sailed together to the seventeenth parallel and then veered apart to separate targets. Depending on the distance, they would arrive on target slightly before or after midnight. Knut, Reidar, and Martin had standing orders that they should prioritize not being detected. Therefore, they should also be out of North Vietnamese territorial waters before dawn. But, as written later about the operations, the Norwegians took the risk of waiting beyond the planned time limit of the rendezvous, until daylight, in the hope of retrieving the raiders on board even when operations had not gone according to plans. According to a recent interview, what they feared most during the operation were airstrikes. However, this sounds unlikely and may be credited to American overcautiousness: at that time, North Vietnam did not have a substantial air force. Maybe American intelligence was unsure about the real status, equipment, location, and readiness of the Vietnam People's Army Air Force; actually, the first fighter unit equipped with MiG-17s would not be transferred from Mengdu, China, their training base, to North Vietnam before August 5, 1964, well after the Vikings were gone. It was also to be considered that the missions were carried out mostly at night, so, at the time, with little chance for any second-rate air force to intervene effectively. But the knowledge of the mere existence of an enemy fighter squadron deployed "somewhere" could probably cause some uneasiness in the American planners.

Normal procedure when the Swifts arrived at the launch point was to stop the engines and switch off whatever else could make noise on board, plus to observe a strict lighting discipline. There was often minimal current and wind, so the Swift would simply drift while they waited.

In some places (such as at the mouth of the Gianh River at Quảng Khê), there was a buoy at the mouth of the river that made it easier to find the drop point. Most of the time it was so dark that they almost had to "feel their way" to the buoy. The drop point was usually 1 to 1.5 nautical miles away from the target. Often, even sounds and noises coming from the land could be heard on board while lying still and waiting in silence.

Although not participating in the missions carried out by the Swifts, the Americans nevertheless were on board during training, conducting tests and rehearsals on the missions. The training was varied. There could be, for example, procedure testing with the Swifts, navigation exercises to improve precision in the dark, unloading and retrieving an inflatable boat, picking up scuba divers when sailing at speed (usually 5–6 knots), and also shooting exercises with the .50-caliber (12.7 mm) machine guns. During these exercises, they often sailed to an island in an uninhabited area where they could fire at will against the mountainside to see the point of impact. Occasionally, they also threw hand grenades, sometimes even into the water to blast fish. Often these exercises, such as pickup at speed, took place right outside the port of Đà Nẵng.

During training the Americans used to test the skills both of the Norwegians and the South Vietnamese in solving their tasks. One such test took place before the first mission in December. The three Vikings all had been sent out to the sea with their respective Swifts to different points and were given the coordinates of a position where they were to reach a buoy dropped beforehand by the Americans. From each respective starting point, they used their sextant to measure the height of the sun to find their own position, then sailed toward where they calculated that the buoy was to be. The one who came closest, or first, would have the "privilege" to take the first real mission. It was Martin who came closest to the buoy and was assigned the first mission.

In addition to exercises and drills, refueling and preparation of the boats were regular tasks. Refueling took place a short distance from the base, up the Hàn River (or Đà Nẵng River, as it was called at the time) in the opposite direction of the base. Occasionally, the boats also had to be docked, for cleaning, painting, and other maintenance. The Vikings docked the Swifts themselves, together with Americans, which after February 1964 were attached to BSU 1 (Boat Support Unit One), originally established by CNO on February 1, 1964.

In general, they worked until late in the evening, and not just on days with missions. On the other hand, they often did not have to start the day too early. The length of the working days varied, but often they had exercises and training with sailing until late in the evening. On weekends, they usually had time off. A favorite recreation place was the beach at My Khe known as "China Beach," west of the Monkey Mountain. It was often both damp and warm, and in their free time they enjoyed a cool "33" beer, a bestseller in South Vietnam.

When operations were carried out with two boats at the same time, each was unaware of the final target and mission of the other.

Knut Kalvenes is convinced that the North Vietnamese knew what was happening, since they had, as is almost certain, informants in place: "They could observe us while we left Đà Nẵng and headed north, but they could not know what we would do once we reached our destination. And they did not know exactly where we were headed." All the Norwegians and South Vietnamese thought that there were infiltrators who passed information to the North about their missions; all too often they had the feeling that they were expected when they got to their targets.

An American intelligence officer said at the time that a Vietcong who had been captured had made an "amazingly accurate" sketch of a Swift boat.

They reached international waters before heading on a northerly course and finally heading toward the coast of North Vietnam.

When they were in North Vietnamese waters, it was in the dead of night. Occasionally they would see lights of a fishing boat or some lights onshore, but otherwise they sailed in complete darkness. The darkness was a friend as well as an enemy.

The Norwegians knew the North Vietnamese coastal radar sites, so the captains used their simple onboard DF (direction-finding) antenna to hone in on the signals that were close to their intended frogman landing sites.

All the landing operations were carried out around midnight. At that hour, a bit before or a bit later, the Swifts would have reached their preplanned positions, a nautical mile off the coast of North Vietnam. The raiders were sent to blow up bridges, ports, or ships or simply to observe strategic positions along the coast.

The four (or more) commandos in the squad, plus any others in support, left in a rubber boat, equipped with explosives, submachine guns (normally M3A1 "Grease Guns" with integral sound suppressor), walkie-talkies, and night binoculars, which could see, on the return leg, the infrared lamp that the Swift boats had on the roof of the wheelhouse in order to help them find their way back to the mother ship.

Hidden offshore in the dark of night, after releasing the assault team, the Norwegians, along with the three crew members, waited in complete silence for the return of the saboteurs. They could speak with each other during the wait, but in whispers. There were enemies around them in the sea, but they didn't know where, because they couldn't hear the silent armed North Vietnamese junks that were on reconnaissance or surveillance missions. To maintain their position, however, every so often they had to start their engines, and each time they risked being discovered. For three or four hours they awaited the return of the raiders with their rubber boats. If all went according to plan, the raiders would return to the Swift around 3:00 in the morning.

Many unexpected situations arose during these operations, says Knut. Everything went well enough until the target was reached, but then they often found out that the situation was different than had been described in the briefing. When the information was not very good, everything became complicated, and risks multiplied. They lost a total of eight commandos whom they transported in various missions.

The first real mission with the Norwegians in command took place on December 15, 1963, a frogman raid (Team NEPTUNE) against the North Vietnamese naval base of Quảng Khê, at the mouth of the Gianh.

This mission was carried out by Martin, but, contrary to what was to be the standard procedure, this time Reidar was also on board. Martin brought the Swift to the drop point, which was at the mouth of the Gianh River (Vietnamese: Sông Gianh), where the North Vietnamese navy base was located. The distance to the base was 1–1.5 nautical miles, and inland there was no light to be seen from the Swift. Although it was dark, you could hear the murmur from the inland when everything on board was turned off. The four frogmen and the support team entered the rubber boat, which was put to sea and headed for the mouth of the river, toward the naval base. The plan was to blow up with limpet mines the North Vietnamese patrol boats lying at the quay in the base. The limpet mines had been put together at the CIA lab on Okinawa. Since the Swatows of that version (P-6, or Project 183 in the Soviet nomenclature) had wooden hulls, the mines had to be modified to attach to the hull by firing a nail into it, like a carpenter's gun, instead of the magnetic clamping. They had a 2-pound TNT charge with a delay clock mechanism. But, as the frogmen approached, they were surprised by a rotating light in the estuary, which revealed two sampans.

The following are details from Thomas Ahern's *The Way We Do Things*:

The last CIA-sponsored maritime sabotage initiative of 1963 reprised the VULCAN operation of 1962 against the North Vietnamese naval base at Quảng Khê. [*Author*: at the time, HQ of the North Vietnamese naval forces in the area, at the mouth of the river Gianh, Quảng Bình Province. The raid conducted the previous year, on June 30, 1962, ended in a disaster; see the chronology in chapter 1, "Before the Vikings."] A Swift, crewed by newly hired [*Author*: omission, probably "Norwegian"] mercenaries, brought the team to the launch point, from which Team NEPTUNE proceeded by rubber boat. A brilliant rotating light at the mouth of the river revealed two sampans, whose occupants challenged the team. The agents saw no way around the sampans, anchored in mid-stream, and fled back to the Swift. Another try on December 23 met a similar fate.

A few days later, on December 23, the mission was to attack the same target as on December 15. Another failed mission, since the course of the mission was quite similar to the December 15 one, according to the CIA report. Apparently, this mission was led by Knut, but Martin clearly remembers having attacked Quảng Khê four times, and the only possibilities to make it up to four are that either he was in command of this mission, too, or that—as a second and last exception to the standard procedure—he accompanied Knut on the Swift.

These offensive efforts began a cycle of alternate operational activities, on the other side, of public trials against operators who had been captured by the North Vietnamese. On December 24, Hanoi announced the trial of "another group of US puppet spy commandos, the tenth since June this year." The six agents in question, belonging to groups that had been infiltrated by parachute, were condemned to sentences varying from five to sixteen years in prison.

DEBATE ON DATES

In an interview from 1985, one of the former South Vietnamese frogmen, Vũ Đức Gương, says that in mid-October 1963 he was on a mission with a Swift in a "support" role, most likely meaning that he was not meant to land but to stay in the rubber boat that was to bring the frogmen toward the target. He says that the operation was interrupted because the captain could not find the drop point for the operation. This operation is not mentioned in any other source. Either it is not on the list of operations because it was aborted before any landing attempt, or it is mixed up with one of the first missions carried out in December 1963. Another possibility is that the missions on December 15 and 23 have been reversed in some of the sources. For example, Martin states the weather was very bad only on the very first mission. Apparently, the failure of the first mission, by all the available reports, was not due to weather conditions, if, as all sources seem to confirm, the first operational mission led by the Vikings was really launched on December 15. Maybe Martin mixes up the memories of that "practice mission" cited by Vũ Đức Gương that placed it in November 1963: there and then the weather conditions forced the mission to be aborted, but it was not the first "live" action. Unfortunately, the only Norwegian keeping a diary, although very sketchy, was Reidar, who started to take notice not before early 1964, and not reporting, understandably, some of the missions and activities in which he was not directly involved. Furthermore, there is the concrete possibility that the South Vietnamese survivors, in recalling events that occurred before or after New Year's Eve, are referring automatically to the Vietnamese Lunar New Year, the Tết, which falls much later than the Western world's new year, usually between the end of January and early February, possibly adding to a misunderstanding.

January 2, 1964

From Reidar's diary: "Knut and Martin docking Swift no. 1."

January 10, 1964

From Reidar's diary: "Cua Viet [*Author*: meaning "exercise on the Cua Viet River," near the border] with observation team. Doc [*Author*: possibly Donald (Doc) Raymond; SEAL Team One], Bus [cover names of

American SEAL instructors/advisers involved in the MAROPS], and Int. [Intelligence? Or another nickname?] "agent team" with 5 persons. Beautiful weather. Launched observation team 1830 and agent team 2100. "Thread" [other nickname that the Norwegians remember for an American], on board as observer. Everything went satisfactorily."

The next day it wouldn't work out as well, and the ensuing exercise (simulated operation) went even worse. From Reidar's diary on January 11: "Approx. 1200. Exercise with air support. 'Red' [nickname for an American adviser] jumped out with a parachute. A drop consisting of a radio for transmission between plane and boat. 'Red' got a very big cut in the forehead. The observation team was unable to get through the surf. Returned to the beach. 'Red' and one of the team swam in to inform Doc and Bus about the air transport mission." "Doc," "Bus," "Thread," and "Red" all are nicknames of Navy SEALS, mostly from SEAL Team One West.

These notes show that the Norwegians trained with the Vietnamese to carry out also reconnaissance and long-range and long-term infiltration in North Vietnam, not just hit-and-run sabotage. The agents could also be landed on the coast, infiltrate, and disappear.

In early January 1964, with the planned takeover of MAROPS by the military, one of the first moves by the Pentagon was to replace the dozen Navy SEALS instructors (Echo Detachment of Navy SEALS Team One, two officers and ten enlisted) who had taken care of the commando and UDT training of the South Vietnamese raiders over the previous year for the CIA, with a new team of twelve Navy SEALS, plus four instructors coming from the US Marines Force Recon. This mixed team was the main structure dedicated to the training within the SOG Maritime Operations Group, better known by the cover name of Naval Advisory Detachment (NAD). Formally, the supervisor was Cmdr. Albert Thomas, an ex-submariner. Tucker Gougelmann, however, due to his experience and expertise, was scheduled to remain in control of the mission planning at least until June. So, as a matter of fact, Albert Thomas acted as nothing more than a liaison officer.

January 14, 1964: Double Mission by Martin and Knut

Three weeks after the aborted mission of December 23, on January 14, 1964, Knut and Martin, with two Swifts, separately landed two teams of commandos (ZEUS and CHARON) at Đồng Hới and 18 kilometers north of it, respectively.

On the afternoon of January 14, Knut and Martin left the White Elephant, where they had spent the night after being briefed on their next mission. They were driven down to the harbor to their respective Swifts. The crew was already on board, and shortly after, the special-forces teams arrived. On board with Martin there would be a team from CHARON, while on board Knut's Swift there would be a team from ZEUS.

The plan this time was more ambitious than the previous ones, and different. One of the targets was a desalinization/pumping station at Bau Tro, on the coast near the city of Đồng Hới, which is the southernmost city of some importance in North Vietnam, north of Đà Nẵng. This target would be attacked by Team ZEUS, embarked with Knut. The second objective was located 18 kilometers north of the base of Quảng Khê and was a ferry that crosses the Ròn River that divides the "Route 1," which is the most important logistic north–south road along the coast. This target would be attacked by Team CHARON, embarked with Martin.

Knut and Martin sailed together north toward the seventeenth parallel. When they crossed the parallel, after dark, as planned they split up, to continue toward their respective targets.

Knut and the team from ZEUS encountered few problems during the mission. When Knut approached land, he stopped the vessel, and the rubber boat was prepared on the stern deck. The assault team entered the dinghy and continued toward the shore. On the beach, they unloaded a "homemade" weapon package made by technicians of the CIA. The package consisted of six 3.5-inch "flat-firing" rockets that were connected to a battery pack. The weapon was aimed at the desalinization station to the best of their ability, and they set the timer. Then they left the place and disappeared on board the rubber boat, to return undetected to the Swift. Knut started the engines and set sail away from the coast. Before Knut's Swift was cruising at full speed, they released some packets of propaganda leaflets floating in the wake as they disappeared into the darkness toward Đà Nẵng.

Martin and the Team CHARON were not so lucky. Less than 19 kilometers from destination, Martin sighted a boat coming toward them from the north. He made some evasive maneuvers and managed to shake off what he perceived to be a pursuer. He arrived at the drop point more than an hour late on schedule. The team leader of CHARON still elected to complete the mission and ordered the team into the inflatable boat. The target was almost a kilometer up the Ròn River, and as they approached

Administrative division of North Vietnam at the time. *CIA*

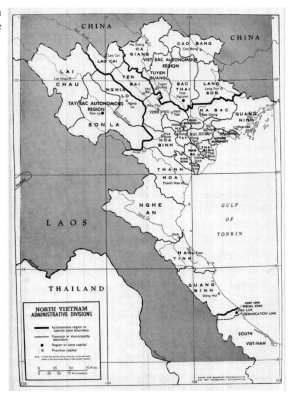

Map of North and South Vietnam, showing the home base of the Vikings, some locations that were the targets of some of their missions, and some targets of later DeSoto missions of the Nasty Boats meant to bombard some North Vietnamese islands.

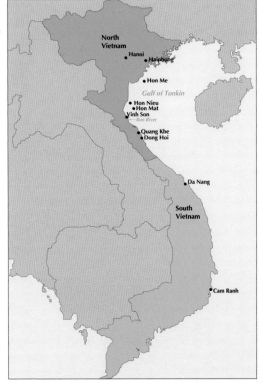

The Hotel Bristol in Bergen, Norway, where the first meeting between Alf Martens Meyer and the three Vikings took place in July 1963. The hotel as it looks today.

Alf Martens Meyer, Norwegian spymaster, and recruiter of the three Vikings upon request of the CIA. He was the organizer of the Norwegian foreign military intelligence after World War II.

The Vikings. *Left to right*: Knut Kalvenes, Martin Vik, and Reidar Steffensen.

BERGEN SJØMANNSKOLE

HØYERE SKIPSFØRERAVDELING 1962/63

Bakerst fra venstre G. Solstad, E. Sjøvangen, K. Stangeland, Overlærer B. Hagland, S. Olsen, E. Olsvik, J. Sætre, P. Mathisen

Midterst fra venstre A. Lyså, R. Steffensen, J. A. Hansen, F. Sjong, H. Hjelde, P. Midbøe, H. Stenberg

Forrest fra venstre P. Rønstad, H. Maurstad, A. Nærøy, Befrakter H. Skare, K. Kalvenes, O. Olsen, G. Johnsen ikke tilstede

Knut Kalvenes graduated from the Bergen Sjømansskole (nautical school) class 1962–63. Knut is second from the right, sitting in first row. Reidar is standing second from the left, central row. *Kalvenes family private collection*

Knut Kalvenes in the graduating class at the Bergen nautical school, academic year 1962–63 (detail taken from class picture). *Kalvenes family private collection*

Reidar Steffensen in the graduating class at the Bergen sail school, academic year 1962–63 (detail taken from class picture). *Kalvenes family private collection*

TASA AIRLINES

ARTURO MULLER A.
PRESIDENT

MICHAEL D. PETROSKY
EXEC. VICE-PRESIDENT
TREASURER

EMILIE S. PETROSKY
SECRETARY

PANAMA, R. P.

CABLE: TUAER

TELEPHONES: 3-4870
RESERVATION 3-7333
3-1180

TOCUMEN 2-2661

P. O. BOX 5056

May 15, 1963

Dear Mr. Knut Kalvenes

T.A.S.A., an airline and general transportation company operating within and out of Panama, has been commissioned by maritime interests in South Vietnam to act as their overseas broker in locating a number of qualified seamen to work in that country.

Through our contacts in shipping circles, your name has been referred to us as a possible interested candidate, and we are writing to determine your availability and willingness to accept employment as a maritime advisor and instructor in Southeast Asia.

Basically, details of the employment contract you will sign in South Vietnam are as follows:

1. The contract salary will be $10,000 a year U.S. or equivalent and you will elect method of payment.

2. Your travel via air will be paid to place of hire and return home with provision for 100 pounds excess baggage. Incidental costs for passports, visas, etc. will be paid by the employer.

3. Meals and lodging or a suitable living allowance will be provided by your employer.

4. The contract death benefit provides $10,000 face value; $10,000 double indemnity for accidental death in performance of duty; and, up to $10,000 health and medical benefits for illness or injury in performance of duty.

5. A normal sick leave benefit not to exceed 14 days per year which is not accruable.

6. A thirty calendar day paid vacation plus travel expenses to and from home if at end of the first contract year it is mutually agreed to contract for a second year.

NO PREGUNTE DONDE VOLAMOS, DIGA DONDE QUIERE IR.

TASA Airlines (CIA front company), preliminary contract proposal for Knut Kalvenes to work in Vietnam, May 1963, first page. *Kalvenes family private collection*

7. You will be an independent contractor and not eligible for benefits other than cited above, i.e., retirement, etc.

8. No dependents will be allowed to accompany or join you.

9. During travel from home to South Vietnam you will be on a retainer fee but benefits above will be in effect.

10. Effective contract date will be upon signing in South Vietnam.

If you find the terms of employment acceptable and can begin work in the near future, please so indicate in order that we may have a firm commitment on your part. We shall then notify your prospective employer and arrangements will be made to facilitate your travel to South Vietnam.

TURISMO AEREO, S. A.

By

Title:

ACCEPTED

TASA Airlines, preliminary contract proposal for Knut to work as a contractor in Vietnam, dated May 1963, second page, with Knut's signature for acceptance. *Kalvenes family private collection*

Đà Nẵng: Martin Vik on the left, Phil Holtz of the CIA in the center, and Reidar Steffensen on the right, together in the villa that hosted the three skippers

Reidar Steffensen posing with an M3A1 submachine gun with M9 flash suppressor, in Đà Nẵng. The Norwegians underwent basic weapons training.

Knut Kalvenes in Đà Nẵng with a sort of colonial fatigues

Another picture of Reidar with an M3A1 submachine gun with flash suppressor, in Đà Nẵng

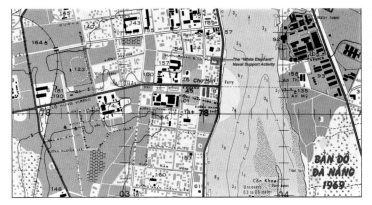

Location of the White Elephant, headquarters of the naval operations, in the center of Đà Nẵng

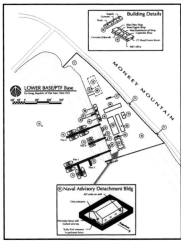

Map of the Swift boat base in Đà Nẵng

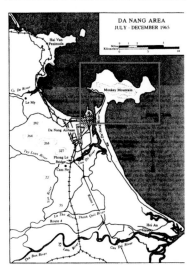

Map of Đà Nẵng, with Monkey Mountain framed in the red square, its internal bay at the base, where the Swifts were moored, and China Beach on the coast just south of it, where most of the training of the South Vietnamese commandos took place

Đà Nẵng in the early 1960s

One of the Viking Swifts in Đà Nẵng Harbor

On the beach, while training

South Vietnamese commando training in Đà Nẵng. *Jim Dunlop via NRK*

South Vietnamese commando training in Đà Nẵng, here with Dennis McCormack, plank owner for SEAL Team One and one of the commando instructors. *Jim Dunlop via NRK*

Entrance gate of Camp Tien Sha, home base of clandestine naval operations in Đà Nẵng, between Marble Mountain and Monkey Mountain, here on October 15, 1965. Judging by the outfit of the sentries, the photo was taken during a thundershower.

The then captain Trương Duy Tài (*second from left*), commander of the Sea Commandos, and the then major Ngô Thế Linh (*second from right*), commander of the Coastal Security Service. *From https://ngothelinh.tripod.com/biethai.html*

Reidar Steffensen, *in the background*, with a team of South Vietnamese commandos that he transported with his fast Swift boat

Navy SEALS instructor Dennis McCormack with two South Vietnamese commandos of Nung ethnicity, Chinese, in Đà Nẵng, 1964, at the time of the Vikings. *From https://www.sealtwo.org/dennismccormack.htm*

South Vietnamese frogmen training. *Jim Dunlop via NRK*

South Vietnamese frogmen
training and preparing for action

South Vietnamese frogmen
training in a rubber boat
preparing for diving

South Vietnamese frogmen
training in the water

South Vietnamese frogmen
training. Recovery phase.

South Vietnamese frogmen training. Trying to recover the diver.

South Vietnamese frogmen training. Trying to make it back to the dinghy.

South Vietnamese frogmen training. Lost the grip; will have to try again.

Moment of relaxation for the Vikings in Đà Nẵng; Reidar Steffensen (*on the left with arms raised*) and Martin Vik (*to the right*)

The White Elephant Building, headquarters of the CIA naval operations

The White Elephant Building

The White Elephant Building

The White Elephant in Đà Nẵng in an aerial picture taken at the time of the Norwegian connection

US Navy SEALS and CIA personnel in Đà Nẵng at the time of the Vikings. Dennis McCormack is the last in the background. Spring 1964. *Jim Dunlop via NRK*

Liên Đội Người Nhái (LDNN), of the South Vietnamese frogmen, here in wetsuit

Probably Knut Kalvenes in Đà Nẵng

Night training for the
South Vietnamese
commandos

South Vietnamese
commando training

South Vietnamese commando training

Viking Swift boats moored at Đà Nẵng

Swift boat below deck. The cots were not needed at the time of the Viking missions.

M3A1 "Grease Gun" with sound suppressor, here with buttstock collapsed. World War II vintage, it was the main weapon of the commandos.

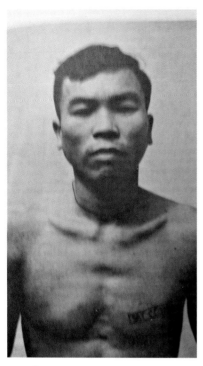

Nguyễn Văn Như, captured on March 12, 1964, when he was leading Team NEPTUNE, of which Vũ Đức Gương was part. *Vietnam News Agency*

Captured South Vietnamese commando Trương Văn Lê, lost in the March 16–17, 1964, mission with Knut Kalvenes on the Swift, showing his equipment in favor of a North Vietnamese camera. On his shoulder is the silenced version of the M3A1 submachine gun. *Vietnam News Agency*

M3A1 "Grease Gun" with sound suppressor, here with buttstock extended. World War II vintage, it was the main weapon of the commandos.

M3A1 "Grease Gun" submachine gun with M9 flash suppressor

the estuary, the swimmers put on their scuba-diving equipment and headed out into the water from the rubber boat. Two of the swimmers continued inward along the northern bank, while two others swam along the southern bank. After a while, they discovered a junk coming down the river. The two swimmers feared that the water was not deep enough for them to get clear of the vessel, and decided to swim back to the rubber boat. The other two swimmers were not to be seen, but the rest of the team was still waiting to see if they would show up. After waiting for the agreed-on time, they left and headed back to Martin's Swift. Daylight was on its way, and Martin realized that he would soon have to get away. Just as he was speeding up the boat, he noticed a flashing light close to the beach. Even though it was very risky, he chose to turn back toward the beach again. To everyone's great relief, it was the last two swimmers who had flashed the light, and he found them close to the shore. The swimmers were taken on board, and Martin set course for Đà Nẵng at full speed.

It's again interesting to go through the details of this mission as reported from the CIA (Ahern 2005): "Three weeks later, on January 14, two Swifts, again manned by [*Author*: omission, probably "Norwegian"] mercenaries, headed north. Team ZEUS would attack a target near Đồng Hới, while Team CHARON headed another 18 kilometers north to take out the Ròn River ferry that served coastal Route 1."[1]

The simpler of the two operations had the better success. Whether it was a desalinization plant, as survivors recalled, or a "Đồng Hới security installation," as reported by the station, it would be hit by rockets fired from the beach, and the hazards of underwater swimming would be avoided. A rubber boat took Team ZEUS ashore, where it succeeded in placing its package of six 3.5-inch rockets, timed for delayed firing. Having pointed the device as best it could, the team returned to the Swift.

The station evaluated its effort as "probably successful."[2]

Team CHARON never reached its target. Delayed by the [*Author*: omission, probably "Norwegian"] captain's evasive maneuvers around a North Vietnamese vessel, it arrived an hour late off the mouth of the Ròn River. Like the agents of Team ZEUS, its two pairs of swimmers left the Swift in a rubber boat. Leaving the boat at the mouth of the Ròn River, two of the frogmen started upstream along the north bank while the other two proceeded along the south. One pair soon encountered a junk and promptly did an about-face back to the rubber boat. There they waited in vain for the other two and finally returned to the Swift. With only half his team back on board, the skipper was about to give up and return to Đà Nẵng when he saw a flashlight blinking near shore. Braving the risk of discovery, he ran the Swift into the shallows, rescued the panicked frogmen, and headed out to sea.[3]

Tit for tat continued on January 28, when Hanoi sentenced the six-man crew of a boat, "sent to cache supplies for doubled Team [omission], to prison terms ranging from 4 to 15 years." This boat crew had nothing to do with the Vikings' operations.

It was one of the last incursions of this type carried out under the aegis of the CIA: since January (although formally since February 1) the MACV-SOG (Military Assistance Command, Vietnam–Special Operations Group, and later Studies and Observation Group) would take charge of these types of mission, without, as we shall see, the approval of the Norwegians. The NAD (Naval Advisory Division) of MACV-SOG, as did the CSS (Coastal Security Service, the parallel South Vietnamese naval service commanded by Major Ngô Thế Linh), had its headquarters located in the "White Elephant Building" in Đà Nẵng.

On February 2, 1964, Gen. William Westmorland, who from the following June would be the commander of American forces in Vietnam, sent a letter to General Khiêm, the minister of defense in Saigon, in which, following the planned acquisition of another six patrol boats (Nasty class), he recommended the recruitment of another forty assault team operators.

February 15, 1964: Another Raid on the Base at Quảng Khê

On February 14, Tucker Gougelmann had summoned Martin for a briefing of the NAD at the White Elephant. [*Author*: Conboy and Andradé reported the briefing as held the very morning of the fifteenth, the same day of the mission; it would be possible, but nonstandard, and very unlikely.] Once again, it was an attack against the North Vietnamese patrol boats in the base of Quảng Khê, and the plan was exactly the same as it had been for the failed attack in December: four combat swimmers, transported by the Swift commanded by Martin, would reach the mouth of the Gianh River. From there, the frogmen would swim up the river to the quays where the vessels are located, and attach limpet mines to the hull.

On February 15, Martin was already on board with the crew when a team of swimmers from Team NEPTUNE arrived at the Swift (Conboy and Andradé report "at noon" the boarding of the four divers, plus the three men in support). Shortly before dark, they left the port of Đà Nẵng and continued out to sea. Just before midnight, they had arrived at the drop point at a buoy at the entrance to the Gianh River, and Martin stopped the engines. The four swimmers and the three support commandos entered the inflatable boat and continued inward to the riverbank. The three support men would remain in the rubber boat to help and keep in touch with the Swift via radio should anything go wrong.

Outside, a fresh breeze was blowing and the sea reinforced, and as the inflatable boat was about to accelerate the surf toward the beach, they were surprised by a strong wave. The rubber boat was lifted and almost capsized, and the men, equipment, and limpet mines fell into the sea. They managed to straighten up the boat and recover the men, terrified. With equipment lost and the engine and radio out of order, they found a couple of reserve oars and tried to find their way back to the Swift. Without radio and infrared light, it looked bleak for the swimmers. They could neither see nor hear the Swift, and the men on board the Swift also had no way to get in touch with the rubber boat. For several hours they paddled around, and the hopes to find the mother vessel were slim, having by now missed the rendezvous time limit. There were instead increasing possibilities to be intercepted by an enemy coast guarder. When daylight began to appear, they saw a vessel approaching. After some moments of suspense, with unimaginable joy they realized it was Martin with the Swift who had found them.

On board the Swift, Martin had realized that something had gone wrong. Since he had not heard gunshots from the beach, he hoped that the swimmers and the inflatable boat had not been discovered. After waiting for a long time, he had to make a choice, since it was nearing dawn. Instead of heading for Đà Nẵng, he took the high risk to stay and sailed from the drop point in "expanding circles" to look for the missing team. In the end, he found them and set course the shortest way out of North Vietnamese waters.

In this mission, one of the commandos recovered by Martin was Vũ Đức Gương, a Team NEPTUNE diver quoted elsewhere in this book. More than thirty years later, Vũ Đức Gương recognized Martin when looking at a picture of the three Vikings.

This mission on February 16, 1964, was allegedly the first "34A boat mission" under the military responsibility, just before the arrival of the first two Nastys. Concerned about the early losses of 34 Alpha program, Ambassador Lodge protested on April 5: "I do not believe any of these missions can be justified except as part of a well-thought-out diplomatic maneuver." Later, Lodge dismissed the MAROPS as good training, perhaps, but having no impact on Hanoi. Adm. U. S. G. Sharp, Pacific commander, blamed inadequate intelligence and an increased state of North Vietnamese alert, making sabotage targets "more difficult to reach than was visualized at the time" (Prados 1986, 48).

February 22–25, 1964: Leisure Trip to Đà Lạt

Having some days off, on February 22 Knut and Reidar took a trip to Đà Lạt, while Martin chose to stay in Đà Nẵng instead. Đà Lạt is a recreational area inland, popular among the Vietnamese as well, where the climate is drier and not quite as hot as in Đà Nẵng. Knut and Reidar had a good time, eating, drinking, and going out to the cinema and to a nightclub. On February 25, they flew back to Đà Nẵng from Đà Lạt.

Two training missions were carried out by Reidar on March 10 and 11, 1964.

MARCH 1964 RAIDS

The uncertainty on the exact dates is particularly puzzling for the month of March. We may say that, historically, it is not a major issue, in reconstructing the general picture, if the real date of a mission was the eleventh or the twelfth. However, given the limited number of sorties, there should be no difficulty in defining a date, with many of the survivors still around and CIA reports and declassified historical essays available. When the doubt was not solvable, I decided to give credit, if and when available, to the dates on the diary kept by Reidar Steffensen in Đà Nẵng. When he writes, on a certain date, "Captain such-and-such returned at X hour, having lost X number of men," it is difficult to find something more reliable. One element can cause discrepancies, besides mistakes and misrememberings: the mission could be recorded, and reported, depending on the source, quoting the day of the briefing (normally one day before the actual departure), the day the Swift boat put to sea, and the day of the return to Đà Nẵng.

March, 12–13, 1964: Fatal Attack at Quảng Khê

On the night of March 12–13, there was a new incursion attempt by Team NEPTUNE, the only one trained for underwater operations, again against the same North Vietnamese base, in order to try to damage the Swatow patrol boats at anchor. The Swift in question was commanded by Martin Vik.

On the afternoon of March 12, Martin was on his way out of the base at Đà Nẵng, again on a mission. After having failed to attack the patrol boats of Swatow type in Quảng Khê on February 15, they will try it again. It is possible that the choice to repeat the attack on the very same target was made because it was assumed that the previous attempt had not been registered by the North Vietnamese, but also because the CIA planners were confident that the more repeated were the attempts against the same place, the more experienced and confident would be the operators, and the more flawless would be the execution. This did not take into account, of course, the alertness and the intelligence and surveillance capabilities of he enemy. This time there were four swimmers from Team NEPTUNE, who would carry out the attack together with three boatmen. The plan was the same as the last time. When they arrived at the buoy at the mouth of the Gianh River, the men entered the dinghy and continued inland toward the mouth of the river. At first everything seemed to go smoothly. Again, the two separate pairs of swimmers headed inland toward the quay, and the agreement was for a rendezvous just outside the quay where the enemy vessels should be located. One in each pair carried the limpet mines, which were held up by a floating sack, while the other carried a board for navigation. Carefully, one pair approached the quay but discovered that there were no vessels there. Nor did they meet the other pair of swimmers. In line with the briefing, the swimmers continued inward toward the alternative quay or Swatow that had been pointed out. Eventually, they hoped to find other "targets of opportunity." They did not find any vessels on the other quay either. Afraid to run out of air in their tanks and not to have enough air to get back to the Swift, they decided to go up on the shoreline. They hid the scuba-diving equipment in some bushes and continued on foot through the jungle to find alternative targets. Before they could get that far, they were shouted at by a patrol, and they realized they had been discovered. They were fired upon but initially managed to hide in the jungle. From the jungle they could hear the noise of the restarted engine from the Swift, but off the beach they also observed North Vietnamese vessels. They realized they could not get back to the Swift. The other two swimmers tried to escape on their own, but one of them was shot on the beach while the other was captured. By the morning of March 15, all three survivors were captured and later sentenced to long prison terms.

On board the Swift, Martin realized, due to the shooting that was heard from the beach, that the swimmers had been discovered. With daylight coming and North Vietnamese vessels in the area, he had no choice but to reluctantly set full speed away from the area and to safety without the swimmers. However, the dinghy with the boat support team was safely on board.

This was also the mission that saw the rescue of frogman Vũ Đức Gương, one of those who survived the earlier missions and North Vietnamese prisons.

March 16–17, 1964: Double Mission

On March 15, Knut and Reidar were separately briefed in the White Elephant for what would be their last mission with targets on land. The MACV SOG-NAD had decided that it was time to stop with the CIA's "fixation" on the underwater attempts against the Swatows at Quảng Khê. The plan this time was relatively complex, and in both missions, much farther north than usual, there were bridges to be blown up. Both bridges were located along Route 1. One was in Kỳ Anh district, in the southern part of Hà Tĩnh Province, while the other was located in Quảng Bình Province. The plans for the two attacks were quite similar. In both rivers, a team of commandos would be employed that would go inward toward the shallow portion of the estuary. From there, four of them would head inland toward the beach, equipped with submachine guns, and act as guards and scouts for the rest of the team, who would wait to go ashore until it was reported that "the coast is clear." Two of the scouts would enter the beach from the inflatable boat to look for North Vietnamese patrols, while the other two would remain in the surf zone outside the beach to look for signals from the first. Eventually, the demolition team would continue ashore to carry out the actual attack on the bridge. According to the plan, they all should be on board the Swift again at 2:00 at night.

So, on the afternoon of March 16,[4] Knut and Reidar set course for the sea from Đà Nẵng together with their respective Swift and crew. As usual when in pairs, they sailed out to sea together, continued north toward the seventeenth parallel, then split up and continued toward their respective targets. On board with Reidar was the usual permanent crew of three, together with a team of nine men from Team CANCER, composed of ethnic Nungs. This team would attack the bridge at Hà Tĩnh.

At the drop-off point, at about 2200, the dinghy was released, and the leader of the team ordered the others into the dinghy. At the transition to the shallow before the beach, they anchored up, and the first four swimmers of the recce team swam their way to shore, with the four of the demolition team waiting on the dinghy for the "go-ahead," together with the ninth man to remain on the rubber boat. Rendezvous with the Swift was fixed at 0200 the next morning. With two men standing by the "surf zone," the two scout swimmers went ashore. They had landed safely on the beach when they discovered that a North Vietnamese foot patrol was coming their way. They bent down, and with the metascope pointing in the direction of the rubber boat, they flashed the danger signal, a double flash. The two men disappeared into the jungle in the hope of not being seen, and of later bringing ashore the others from the rubber boat, as planned. However, the patrol had seen the traces in the sand after them, and the two Nungs of the scout section, Voong A Cầu and Châu Heng Xương, hiding in the jungle, were captured after four days.[5] The rest of the team turned quickly, got in the rubber boat, and managed to get on board the Swift again. Reidar, after waiting for a long time beyond the planned rendezvous, sped it up and was forced to return to Đà Nẵng without the two unlucky swimmers. He arrived at Đà Nẵng at 1200 in the afternoon on March 17.

A little earlier in the evening, Knut arrived at the drop point outside the target in Quảng Bình. The plan was similar to the one followed by Team CANCER of the parallel mission, and this team managed to get the first two men ashore on the beach. Casually, they ran into a group of fishermen, who alerted the security forces. The two commandos tried to escape toward the interior (while the rest of the group got safely back to the boat) but quickly realized that they had been discovered. After a manhunt, the North Vietnamese foot patrols managed to find them. The pair was in radio contact with the Swift, but there was nothing that could be done to save them. One of the two commandos was shot in the ensuing firefight, while the other, Trương Văn Lê, was captured and later obliged to pose for North Vietnamese cameras showing the mission equipment. The rest of the team managed to get back on board the Swift. Like Reidar, Knut, after waiting for long past the rendezvous time limit, had to return to Đà Nẵng and report the loss of two swimmers, arriving to the home base at 10:00 in the morning of the seventeenth.[6]

As previously mentioned, Reidar's notebook covers only the 1964 operations, but even in 1964, not all operations are recorded. The operations on January 14 and February 15 are not reported, most likely because they were carried out by Knut and Martin. Not being involved, Reidar was obviously kept separate from the other two.

Reidar does not report missions on March 11–12, but on the twelfth and thirteenth. The dates from the various sources (CIA, Tourison, Conboy and Andradé, and relevant interviews to the veteran frogmen) can cause some confusion because, as said, let alone possible misrememberings, it can be misleading whether they refer to the starting date of the mission or the end date. Reidar has noted for the March 12–13 mission that "Mike" (Martin) had an operation during which he lost all four swimmers. He actually did not return before 1300, indicating that Martin took a great risk, again, to search for the missing men even in daylight. Wick Tourison reports four "frogmen," quoting each of them by name, as lost on March 12, 1964. Interviewed by Tourison in 1989, Vũ Đức Gương reports to have been captured on the mission of March 12, but this surely refers to the starting date of the mission. Anyway, Vũ Đức Gương, in his attempt to flee with his comrade, heard the firefight that he later found out was caused by the operation on March 15, which was not conducted by the Vikings, and he is said (if there is no typo error in the transcript) to have been captured with his comrade on April 15, which is surely a mistake for March 15, also because he specifies that it was one of his captors who told him about this new attempt on March 15. Other parallel clandestine coastal operations were going on at the time: harassment, reconnaissance, or resupply to long-term teams previously infiltrated by sea or air, carried out by the South Vietnamese or by the Americans, using the still-existing junk force. Thus, in the overlapping or near overlapping of missions, dates, and human losses, especially after the acceleration due to the military takeover of the operations, it's not always easy to define who did what and when.

Reidar, asked about other foreign nationals involved, said that he remembered that both Taiwanese and Germans had been involved in the operations, but for the Germans it was the "Gassers," not the Swifts or the Nastys. Hamilton, in mentioning "a dozen" Norwegians, may of course confuse Germans and Norwegians, Swifts and Nastys. Reidar remembered that the Nastys arrived in early 1964, but he also said that there were "closed walls between the different groups, and they knew little about each others' operations."

Several US sources seem to indicate that apart from the Vikings on the Swifts, there were Norwegians involved with a supporting role for the Nastys. The time frame from the purchase of the first two Nastys, PTF 03 (originally *Skrei* for the Royal Norwegian Navy) and PTF 04 (formerly *Hvass* for the RNN), the show-off in the US, and the final delivery in Đà Nẵng (via Pearl Harbor and Subic Bay, Philippines) may seem too short for the US to have built competence, logistics, and repair facilities completely on their own. However, James "Jim" Hawes, one of the CIA/SEAL officers in Đà Nẵng, who was second in command of mission planning starting in May 1964, replacing Phil Holtz (who had the same role from mid-1963 to mid-1964), has confirmed that there were no Norwegian mentors or advisers for the Nastys after the stopover in Pearl Harbor. On the other hand, it is confirmed that personnel from the Mandal Dockyard (A/S Westermoen Båtbyggeri shipyard, located in Mandal, Norway) and Norwegian navy at least supported the logistic side in Subic Bay.

Reidar also confirms that there were no Germans tested on the Swifts before the Vikings arrived. But he also knew that the Germans on the Nastys [*Author*: we know it was the "Gassers"] were sent off due to their alcohol consumption and trouble around them, confirming the story of the five Germans recruited by the CIA station in Bonn; the "Gasser" Germans proved to be totally ineffective and were repatriated.

March 23, 1964: Birth

Reidar receives a telegram with this good news: "Congratulations! You are now the father of a healthy newborn daughter."

May 27, 1964: LOKI Mission, Seizure of a North Vietnamese Junk

The last mission with the Norwegians in command was carried out on May 27, 1964, and it had the objective to capture in full daylight a fishermen's junk to interrogate the crew on Cù Lao Chàm Island ("Paradise Island," a beautiful island some 12 nautical miles off Đà Nẵng), essentially to get information on targets and defenses at Đồng Hới, plus to administer some political indoctrination and propaganda.

It would be Reidar with Swift no. 3 to accomplish the last mission performed by the Norwegian skippers. The plan briefed at the White Elephant this time was completely different from the previous ones. It was to be a bold daylight LOKI mission, which in short meant a kidnapping. The plan was for the Swift to sail out at night and enter North Vietnamese waters at some usual fishing areas. In full daylight, they would then capture and kidnap a North Vietnamese junk with its fishermen. The junk and the fishermen would be taken to Đà Nẵng, and then the fishermen would be taken out to the island of Cù Lao Chàm for interrogation and indoctrination. Carrying this out in full daylight was risky, and one of the newly arrived Norwegian Nasty-class PTFs would follow in the background for protection.

Late at night on May 27, Reidar sailed from Đà Nẵng toward a fishing area outside Đồng Hới in Quảng Bình Province. While investigating the fishing vessels from a distance, Reidar picked out an isolated junk in the outskirts of the fishing grounds. Reidar quickly got alongside the junk, and the team of special forces stormed on board. According to Reidar there was no trouble during the boarding, since none of the fishermen were armed. The North Vietnamese fishermen were terrified, and one of them peed in his pants. All six fishermen were taken on board the Swift and blindfolded; they were stowed in a corner below deck. It was important that Reidar was not seen, since he was the only non-Vietnamese on board. Then some sailors from the crew on the Swift were put on board the junk, and it was towed to South Vietnamese waters. There was no fighting or exchange of fire in connection with the hijacking. The commandos were armed, and the fishermen were not. As soon as the Vietnamese junk was towed away from the fishing field and out of sight, a Nasty boat came and accompanied the tow for safety. After passing seventeenth parallel, the fishermen were transferred to a motorized junk and sailed directly to the island of Cù Lao Chàm, while Reidar continued back to Đà Nẵng with the kidnapped junk in tow.

"It's been risky," Reidar remembers, "but it worked out rather well. We came alongside the sampan and boarded it. There was no noise, and none of the fishermen were armed. All the fishermen, maybe four or five [*Author*: the American source quotes six fishermen, and this time they are probably more reliable than Reidar's memories], were transferred on the Swift. We then had some of our crew to man the captured sampan and towed it into South Vietnamese waters. There were no handshakes, but no one put up a fight during the kidnapping. Our commandos were armed, and they weren't. The poor fishermen were captured, literally pissed off." [*Author*: in the other abovementioned interview, Reidar described them as "terrified"; we may well say that one thing does not exclude the other.] As soon as the Vietnamese sampan was in safe waters, a Nasty boat came and ensured further escort and security to the convoy.

The island of Cù Lao Chàm is a story in itself. On this island, which the CIA called "Paradise Island," the CIA had set up a fake village where South Vietnamese who had fled from North Vietnam were used as actors. The actors gave the impression that there was a North Vietnamese anti-Communist resistance movement called the SSPL (Sacred Sword of the Patriots League, recalling the struggle of the Vietnamese against the Chinese Ming dynasty), and that they were preparing for war against the regime in North Vietnam.

The interrogation of the fishermen lasted for two days and was conducted mainly by a South Vietnamese captain (a Catholic northerner by origin, so with the "right" accent) disguised as a member of the SSPL, and the translation in English for MACV-SOG was provided by Sgt. David Elliott, a US Army linguist hastily mobilized from Saigon while still wearing black pajamas, armed with a Swedish submachine gun, and whisked to the island, supposedly the "support headquarters" of the SSPL. After two days the six fishermen were released where they had been seized, with gifts and propaganda material.

They were taken up north to the seventeenth parallel on a motorized junk and then again transferred to the Swift, which brought them farther north to a fishing area in North Vietnamese waters, with a Nasty-class PTF towing the kidnapped junk. With the Nasty class out of sight, the fishermen were transferred from the Swift to their own boat. They were given food, gifts, propaganda materials, and "wishes for good luck" (even a guitar), and then the Swift disappeared back to Đà Nẵng, with the Nasty as a distant escort. Some sources (e.g., Moïse 1996) place the release of the fishermen on June 2.

Reidar got the impression that those fishermen had been treated well. "After the interrogation, they were released and presented some gifts; they looked rather happy," adds Reidar. We may say that maybe they were happy to have been released. None of the Norwegians knew of this setup and program, but now all of it is well known, thanks to various sources, including interviews with the ex-director of the CIA William Colby,[7] who at that time was head of the Far East Division of the agency.

On June 1964, the Norwegians did not further extend their contract, and on the sixteenth they were repatriated. The takeover of the missions by the military was not appreciated by the Vikings, who liked the mission management of the CIA, particularly from the security point of view. [*Author*: Quách Rạng, a former deputy commander of a parachute commando team involved in the airborne missions, said in an interview released in 1993 to Sedgwick Tourison that with the military takeover of the clandestine operations, the parachute teams were gathered together at Long Thanh and no longer kept strictly separated as it had been before. All the members got to know the others, their accents, and their areas of origin, and of probable employment in the North. Furthermore, they learned that until then, nobody who had been sent in a mission had made it back. In short, they found out too much, and security was compromised; morale dropped too. Although the case is not directly connected with the naval operations examined here, it provides a basic idea of the low consideration by the MACV-SOG of the security aspects, sacrificing everything to the numbers of missions to produce, although the CIA officers in Đà Nẵng somehow kept managing the MAROPS at least until summer 1964.]

In the original letter of recommendation, dated June 15, 1964, drafted and delivered in the HQ of the CSS in Saigon and released to Knut (but I believe a letter was drafted for each of the three Norwegians) with high praise at the end of the year of contract in Vietnam, there is the stamp and signature of a certain "Major Nguyen Binh, Chief of the CSS Coastal Security Service ARVN, Saigon," which was none other that the secret alias, the covert name, of Major Ngô Thế Linh, the chief of CSS, established since April 1, 1964, in place of the former CSF.[8]

In hindsight, one cannot help remarking that the South Vietnamese volunteers of the special forces—mostly destined to death or, at best, long-term captivity in a North Vietnamese prison—saw their missions as something very patriotic for which to risk their life. Vice versa, for the White House, the Pentagon, and the CIA, they were just expendable pawns in operations bound for almost sure disaster, in the complex game of "trying to do something" to fulfill the expectations of the political and military authorities in Washington.

The American military authorities declared the lost commandos presumably dead, even when there were reports or evidence of their existence in North Vietnamese prisons. In this way, they could stop paying the promised fees to their families, plus it helped in hiding these covert operations. After the Paris Peace Accords in 1973, the United States was busy getting their POWs or MIAs back home, and the South Vietnamese commandos were not their top priority. The government of Saigon, during the war, did not (or could not) recognize them as working for South Vietnam; after April 1975 they simply ceased to exist. So, in the end, no one reclaimed them.

On June 16, 1964, with their six-month contract having expired, the Norwegians returned home. The handoff from CIA management to the MACV-SOG military officers was not looked upon positively by the Vikings, who were comfortable with the guidance and preparation of the missions by the CIA, especially from the security standpoint, while the MACV-SOG management was much different. Because of that, they decided not to renew their contract.

All three of the Norwegians, as we have seen, sooner or later, lost some commandos during their cycle of operations; Martin Vik lost four commandos in one mission. Martin had heard shooting from the beach and thought that all of them had been hit (we now know that only one was killed, and the others were captured). Reidar Steffensen and Knut Kalvenes each lost two raiders. They knew nothing of their fate and suffered over it, because despite the difficulties due to language, over time they had become friends. This had been especially difficult for Knut, because on the night between March 16 and 17, he had been able to hear the two raiders over the walkie-talkie while they tried desperately to find his patrol boat. Despite the infrared lamp, and despite the fact that they had radio contact, it was impossible for the commandos to find their direction in the dark. For half an hour, Kurt waited for the Vietnamese before ordering to put about. He had barely enough time to escape before daybreak set in. On the morning of March 13, Martin had lingered even longer before returning to Đà Nẵng.

In Reidar's diary of March 17, 1964, he says, "Knut came back at 1000. He had lost two swimmers. Probably killed. I returned at 1200. I lost two swimmers. Reason unknown." Martin had lost his four swimmers the day before (March 12–13). Part of these operations consisted of infiltrating agents into the North, and it was therefore possible that some of the naval raiders were destined to "disappear" without the Norwegians having been notified.

The author and researcher John Prados, who studied these operations without discovering the details of the Norwegian participation (until his meeting with this author in Philadelphia at a conference held on February 10, 2016, where Prados was one of the honored guests, as well as at a very convivial dinner the following evening), states that until July 1964 the sabotage raids had three successes: destruction of a bridge on Highway 1, partial destruction of a warehouse, and temporary shutdown of a hydraulic pumping station.

These operations had a negative outcome from whatever aspect one looks at them. If Kennedy's objective was, as others maintain, from a certain point and later had become to provoke the North Vietnamese to create a casus belli and thus be able to unleash a large-scale war, it can be said that it succeeded partially (the North Vietnamese leaders initially absolutely did not give the Americans a pretext for a direct intervention), so much so that in the end it was necessary to rely on an incident that did not really happen (the Tonkin incident of August 4, 1964) to force Congress's hand, but the war that followed dragged South Vietnam and the United States into the disaster that we know. Neil Sheehan, in his book *A Bright Shining Lie*, maintains that the 34 Alpha operations were used by President Johnson as a principal pretext to provoke the war.

When the increasing scope and the increased dangers associated with these operations became evident in the eyes of the Norwegians, the nostalgia for home also was reawakened. When the Americans made an offer to continue "in the work," they consulted among themselves. "We sat down one night," says Knut, "we talked about it, and we realized that morally we could no longer have a part in this. We knew that the situation down there was leading to war." When they informed the Americans of this, there was no problem. "They tried to make us stay, and they offered us a higher salary, but we had decided," says Knut. They also called Martens Meyer in Norway and told him they wanted to return home, and Martens Meyer did not try to impede their return.

June 1964: Homecoming

The contract period for the three Norwegians lasted theoretically until August. As a replacement for the three Norwegians, the Americans hired eight Chinese captains from Taiwan. These were Taiwanese navy officers who had previous experience with fast patrol boats. With very good feedback from both NAD and the South Vietnamese, however, the Americans had obviously preferred Martin, Knut, and Reidar to stay and extend their term. They were therefore asked if they would like to go over to the Nasty class, as a sort of upgrade. Martin replied that he, strictly speaking, did not have a certificate to sail these boats, and rejected the offer. The truth is that Martin and the others were more than qualified for such a task. Americans settled down with this answer. When Martin rejected the offer, the others also decided not to continue. Even offers of higher wages did not make them change their mind. There is more than one reason why they did not extend the contract. The shift from CIA to the military was one of the main points. The CIA's role in the operations gradually diminished from February onward, and both Reidar and Martin say that the US Navy managed things differently than the CIA, in a way they did not appreciate: more operations, larger operations, tighter command and control, and, last but not least, greater risk. In addition, the loss of crew from some of the operations affected them. The Norwegians say that they liked CIA's smaller-scale approach better, and the security aspects were much better handled than by the military. On June 16, after they had received their brilliant certificates on behalf of the Americans, they started the journey home from Đà Nẵng, via Saigon and Paris to Norway.

THE LAST MEETING WITH ALF MARTENS MEYER

A few weeks after returning home, they were invited home by Martens Meyer for a chat. None of them remember in detail what happened at this meeting, but in earlier interviews, Reidar and Knut have said that it did not take the form of a debriefing. It was more of a nice social gathering, where they talked a lot about their experiences in Đà Nẵng. Maybe Martens Meyer purposefully kept it on the informal side. The mission of Knut, Martin, and Reidar had, in principle, nothing to do with the Norwegian authorities. It is also possible that in downplaying it all, Meyer may have instilled in the three sailors the feeling that what they had been involved in was not that much of a big deal, so nothing to brag about and spread as exciting news.

Meyer, who was still organizing the Norwegian ELINT and SIGINT, mainly an anti-Soviet perspective, called Martin Vik a while after his return to give him the command of the ELINT/SIGINT ship *Marjata*, a command that Vik reportedly held at least until the year 2000(!).

Notes

1. Kenneth Conboy and Dale Andradé, *Spies and Commandos: How America Lost the Secret War in North Vietnam* (Lawrence: University Press of Kansas, 2000), 72–73. The CIA station report says that Team ZEUS should have hit a not-better-specified "security installation" at Đồng Hới.

2. CIA Saigon station report, SAIG3823, January 16, 1964.

3. Conboy and Andradé, *Spies and Commandos*, 93. The missions passed from the CIA to the DoD. To manage them, the MACV created the special-operations group MACV-SOG, under Col. Clyde Russell. Also see Sedgwick Tourison, *Secret Army, Secret War* (Annapolis, MD: Naval Institute Press, 1995).

4. The sources covering these missions are inaccurate or unclear as to dates. In Conboy and Andradé's book *Spies and Commandos*, two separate missions are described on March 15 and 17, respectively. Tourison, in his book *Secret Army, Secret War*, mentions these missions very briefly, without indicating dates. On the other hand, he has a list of swimmers who were lost, and here are mentioned two separate pairs of swimmers reported as lost on March 15. A list of NAD's missions in March 1964 lists two separate missions completed by Swift boats on March 16. In his diary, Reidar Steffensen writes on March 17: "Knut returned 1000. Lost 2 swimmers. Probably shot. I returned 1200. Lost 2 swimmers. Reason unknown." So, the evidence is that two separate missions were carried out on the very same night, between March 16 and 17, at two different locations with Swifts commanded by Knut and Reidar. Tourison reports two members of Team CANCER, quoting them by name, as lost on March 15, 1964, and another two members of an "unknown" team, although known by name, lost on the same date. Again, the doubt derives from whether he refers to the start date or the end date of the mission, but we do know that on March 15, there was a parallel operation not connected to the Vikings.

5. In the spring of 1978, fourteen years later, Voong A Cầu, with a prison mate, Lê Trung Tín, belonging to a different team and different mission, managed to escape from the prison of Hong Thang, joining a mass evasion organized by common criminals detained there, reaching China together with some other Taiwanese commandos equally escaped, and with the thieves of the gang whose leader had organized the evasion. They were the only South Vietnamese—and as a matter of fact, the only Southern Allied military, among Americans, Allied, and South

Vietnamese—to escape successfully from a prison camp in North Vietnam, although to end up in Communist China.

6. Apparently, the night of March 15, during the raid on Quảng Bình Province by the coastal assault group (heard by Vũ Đức Gương on the run), saw the use of 57 mm recoilless rifles. Of the two commandos captured on the beach, one, Nguyễn Văn Sắc, was an ex-military of the Union Française at the time of the French Indochina War. This didn't help his case; he would be tried, sentenced to death, and shot the following July.

7. William Colby, who later became director of the CIA between 1973 and 1976, in his wartime service with the OSS, had come across Norway and its clandestine services. RYPE was the code name for an American parachute force, the Norwegian Special Operations Group (NORSO). On March 24, 1945, the group, with eight four-engine B-24 planes, left RAF Harrington airport in England and parachuted over Snåsafjella (Operation Grouse). The operation established a base at Gjefsjøen mountain farm by the frozen lake of Gjevsjøen (or Gjefsjøen, Swedish: Jävsjön), on the border between Norway and Sweden, in the southern part of central Norway. In 1959, Colby became the CIA's deputy chief of station and then chief of station in Saigon, where he served until 1962. Colby established a relationship with President Diệm's family and with Ngô Đình Nhu, the president's brother. While in Vietnam, Colby focused on building up Vietnamese capabilities to combat the Vietcong insurgency in the countryside. He argued that "the key to the war in Vietnam was the war *in* the villages." [*Author*: as opposed to the "war *on* the villages."] In 1962 he returned to Washington to become the deputy and then chief of CIA's Far East Division. During these years, Colby was deeply involved in Washington's policies in East Asia, particularly with respect to Vietnam (Phoenix Program), as well as Indonesia, Japan, Korea, and China. He was deeply critical of the decision to abandon support for Diệm, and he believed that this played a material part in the weakening of the South Vietnamese position in the years following.

8. A brief summary on the formation and the missions of the Coastal Security Service (CSS). The Northern Department, under Captain Ngô Thế Linh, belonged to the Presidential Liaisons Office (an intelligence unit) from 1959 to 1963 and had two teams responsible for clandestine missions by air/land and by sea, and they were stationed at Huế and Đà Nẵng: (1) the so-called Atlantic Team, stationed at Huế city, for infiltrations by air/land, and (2) the so-called Pacific team at Đà Nẵng, for infiltrations

from the sea. After the November 1963 coup d'état that overthrew Diệm, South Vietnam special forces expanded and moved to a new base in Nha Trang. It then became Vietnamese Commandos Department, reporting to the Vietnamese armed forces chief of staff. At this time, Coastal Security Service (CSS) was established on April 1, 1964. The Northern Department's Pacific and Atlantic teams then merged into CSS. CSS conducted all sea commandos attack missions beyond the seventeenth parallel, into North Vietnam. Commander Ngô Thế Linh was the first CSS commander in April 1964. By the end of 1962, United States sent two patrol boats with two naval commanders. However, CSS sailors were composed mainly of Vietnamese, recruited and trained by the South Vietnamese government. The first eighteen South Vietnamese trained as combat scuba divers, however, had received a four-month training by American instructors in Taiwan as early as 1960, returning home in December the same year. Of this group, the one officer and seven men coming originally from the South Vietnamese navy formed the first frogman unit. After a slow beginning, CSS personnel increased rapidly after April 19, 1964, creating new teams. The US Navy also sent a SEAL Team (ATHENA) to advise and train Vietnamese sea commandos, with CSS first commando team commanded by Lieutenant Ninh Nhut Lam. In addition, Ensign Hùng and Ngô commanded another team (ROMULUS) that comprised fifty members, all coming from the South Vietnamese marines. The remaining SEAL teams were as follows: Teams CHARON and ZEUS which later that summer would be merged in a new single team named CUMULUS, Team CANCER (ethnic Nungs), who remained since it was also under MACV-SOG management; Team NEPTUNE, the sole scuba-diving team, which after the heavy losses was progressively inactivated; Team VEGA (with personnel drawn from the South Vietnamese paramilitary junk force); and Team NIMBUS (ARVN rangers and airborne). Hung Ho, Ngô Thế Linh's son, lists six SEAL teams: MERCURY, ROMULUS, CUMULUS, NIMBUS, VEGA, and CANCER, thus considering Team ATHENA as a South Vietnamese unit and not the US Navy SEAL advisory team as reported by Conboy and Andradé (though it could probably be an advisory team later turned into a SVN unit), and adds Team MERCURY, not mentioned by Conboy & Andradé. In any case, the development of these teams brings us far beyond the time frame in which the Norwegians performed their missions. Robert Sullivan, a.k.a. "Chief Sullivan," for his part, referring to the training of the South Vietnamese frogmen, wrote: "Their training was in open-circuit SCUBA only, and that is the only equipment we will have to use for a Limpet mine attack on the Swatows. Obtaining closed-circuit gear and training the frogmen in its use is out of the time period planned for the completion of the operation."

CHAPTER
5

After the
Vikings

After the departure of the Norwegians on June 16, the operations beyond the seventeenth parallel went on, at least initially, with eight Taiwanese skippers who literally took the place of the Norwegians (same location, same villa in Đà Nẵng). Even the Taiwanese were, at least for a while, still referred to by the Americans as the Vikings.

Originally, the Taiwanese were meant to be transferred later from the Swifts to the bigger Nastys, but, after the South Vietnamese crews qualified for the Nastys, and the Chinese proved to be less skilled in seafaring than was initially thought, they remained on the Swifts until the end of their tour of duty. After the Taiwanese, the fast boats were manned by totally South Vietnamese crews, and, on the other hand, the Americans became more and more involved in the missions, even before the official "green light" from Washington. Taiwanese elements, or more often ethnic Nung Vietnamese, participated to the missions, in order to have personnel familiar with the North Vietnamese areas populated by Nungs, and to have Chinese-speaking people who could interrogate captured Chinese advisors (this happened at least in one case).

Chronology of the incursions immediately after the repatriation of the Norwegians

July 7, 1964. Kidnapping of three North Vietnamese fishing boats, to bring the fishermen onto Paradise Island, off Đà Nẵng, for interrogation and indoctrination; subsequently they were released with propaganda material and gifts.

July 20, 1964. Kidnapping of two North Vietnamese fishing boats, to bring the fishermen onto Paradise Island for interrogation and indoctrination; subsequently they were released with propaganda material and gifts.

July 30–31, 1964. South Vietnamese commandos carry out a surprise attack on two North Vietnamese islands in the Gulf of Tonkin (Hòn Mê and Hòn Ngư [Hòn Niêu]) believed to be support bases for enemy infiltration. Simultaneously, these same islands are bombarded by South Vietnamese naval units (Norwegian-made Nasty-class patrol boats). The US destroyer USS *Maddox* (DD-731), on an ELINT mission, waits 123 nautical miles south, for the purpose of electronically simulating an air attack to stop North Vietnamese naval units from counterattacking the South Vietnamese amphibious force.

August 2, 1964. Three North Vietnamese 123K-class motor torpedo boats (sub-version equipped with radar of the Soviet type P-4, 3rd Division [section] of the 135th Motor Torpedo Boat Battalion [Squadron]) attack, without consequences, USS *Maddox* while it is engaged in an ELINT electronic reconnaissance "DeSoto" mission. A subsequent US air attack by four F-8 Crusaders from the aircraft carrier USS *Ticonderoga* damages the North Vietnamese units, in part heavily, possibly sinking one.

August 3–4, 1964. Three Nasty gunboats of the South Vietnamese navy bombard (Operation 34A) the mouth of the Ròn River (or Sông Roòn) and the radar at Vĩnh Sơn, in North Vietnam.

August 4, 1964. "Gulf of Tonkin incident." The US destroyer USS *Maddox*, on an electronic-surveillance mission together with USS *C. Turner Joy*, identifies North Vietnamese torpedo boats in the area. In a confused situation, amid false radar echoes and misinterpreted sonar signals, *Maddox* reports that it has been attacked by North Vietnamese ships. The two destroyers maneuver and fire for two hours against radar signals mistaken for enemy ships.

August 5, 1964. Operation Pierce Arrow: US naval aviation aircraft based on the aircraft carriers USS *Ticonderoga* and USS *Constellation* conduct sixty-four sorties against North Vietnamese torpedo boat bases in Hòn Gai, Loc Chao, Quảng Khê, and Bến Thủy, and a fuel depot in Vinh. Two aircraft are shot down by antiaircraft artillery: a Douglas A-1 Skyraider, whose pilot is killed, and a McDonnell Douglas A-4C Skyhawk, whose pilot, Lt. j.g. Everett Alvarez Jr., ejects and becomes the first American pilot to be taken prisoner in Vietnam. US pilots report the destruction of 90 percent of Vinh's fuel depots and the sinking or damaging of twenty-five P-4-class motor torpedo boats. This mission marks the beginning of US air operations over North Vietnam, and Southeast Asia in general, aimed at destroying infrastructure, materials, and military units needed by North Vietnam to supply the guerrillas in the South.

August 7, 1964. On the basis of the impression given by the reports on the "Tonkin Gulf incident," the US Congress passes the "Tonkin Resolution," which gives President Johnson free rein regarding the defense of American forces and bases in the area, and the use of any force deemed necessary to support South Vietnam in its struggle. The result in the Senate is 88 to 2, and in the House 416 to 0.

A final consideration is due on the strategic result of these missions. As for what was expected by the Americans, it was exactly the opposite. Far from being intimidated, worried, and "enforced" by this "payback" for their activities and infiltrations in the South, the North Vietnamese had the evidence, substantiated by the capture of many enemy commandos, needed by their propaganda, that it was America's long arm that was bringing war to their home, saying to their people and convincing their people that it was a just cause and a necessity to join the army to go fighting in South Vietnam.

CHAPTER 6

The Memories

Knut Kalvenes and Reidar Steffensen were interviewed shortly before 2000, while Martin Vik, who had long commanded the Norwegian spy and ELINT/SIGINT ship *Marjata*, refused to be interviewed since he was still in service with the Norwegian intelligence service. He was later interviewed by telephone by the author and Jan Tore Nilsen.

Knut Kalvenes, later to enjoy a brilliant career as a businessman and involved in local politics, tells the story in the accent of the fjords of the Norwegian western south-central coast: "The night before our first mission in Vietnam, they gave us a briefing: tomorrow certain people are coming. At the appointed hour, they came, in cars or jeeps, we loaded them, and we weighed anchor. The South Vietnamese were saboteurs and recon personnel. They always worked at night." Speaking of Meyer, he says, "I understood only later [after Vietnam], watching television, that Alf Martens Meyer was a big shot in the Norwegian intelligence service." He also maintains that, given the mode and scope of the contact, as far as he knows there was no reason for the Norwegian government to be informed. It was all very simple and informal; the Americans went to Meyer, asking him if he knew people with those qualifications, and he did nothing more than find the right people, marrying up a request and an offer. He remembers: "We didn't have strong ideological convictions; we were generally pro-American; we didn't think much about what we were doing was right or not. We asked ourselves some questions later, with the development of the war in Vietnam in the years that followed."

Reidar Steffensen, on the other hand, found the meeting with Meyer at the Hotel Bristol to be very secret. Meyer did not explain who he was or whom he represented; he said only that he could arrange for this work in South Vietnam. They signed a contract that explicitly stated that they accepted the risk of being "killed in action." With respect to a clause that family could not be invited to visit them, the reason seems to have been the fear that family might talk them into returning home.

At the time, none of the three, with the possible exception of Martin, knew that Meyer was a very highly placed officer in the Norwegian secret service. They understood it quickly enough after they arrived in Vietnam.

"We were almost employees," says Reidar. "Meyer was our manager. We had contact with him only in Norway, not with anyone else." Meyer had made a good impression on the three sailors, who described him as "good company."

Knut said, "I remember him as if it were today, with a plain jacket and pants." There was nothing to indicate that he was so high in the intelligence organization.

Knut Kalvenes remembers: "Only once," he said, "I've lost some men, far to the north [March 16–17, 1964, mission]. We had to be out of the [NVN] territorial waters before dawn, and we had a problem due to the distance, given the long time needed to go all our way up and back. We had only half an hour to make it to the international waters. So we told the commandos that this time they had to make it on their own back to the mother boat waiting aloof. I felt so sorry because we had become friends. We never heard of them again."

Knut passed away in January 2015. The author contacted his widow and son, who have been very kind and helpful.

Reidar Steffensen, with a typical Bergen accent, in a somewhat cryptic manner, instead says, "They knew about us; it was useful for them that we were there, both because we were a Norwegian 'antenna' in a far-off place as well as because our presence was 'discreet.'" It is not clear who he is referring to with the "they," but it seems obvious that he is referring to the intelligence service or to the Norwegian governmental structure.

Reidar Steffensen is now relaxed and at ease in talking about this adventure, but for about thirty years after his return, he had some nerve problems and difficulty in concentration.

He now depicts himself and his two mates as a sort of "three musketeers": they were looking for adventure, action, exotic lands, and freedom.

The third member of the team, Martin Vik, was long silent. The reason is that he was still working for the Norwegian secret service. Martin was the captain of the spy ship *Marjata* and was officially employed by the armed forces research institute, but in reality he was like the others aboard the ship under the command of the E-tjenesten. For reasons of privacy or security, Martin changed his surname from Vik to Øyerhavn.

The *Marjata* is one of the most important COMINT/SIGINT assets of the Norwegian intelligence service, active mainly in the Barents Sea. In reality, there are four ships that, successively, have functioned in the role and assumed the name *Marjata*. Alf Martens Meyer is the man who "created" the *Marjata*. Like the rest of the crew aboard the *Marjata*, Øyerhavn was selected for this work directly by Martens Meyer. The reason why Øyerhavn got the job was most probably because of his performance in Vietnam, from which he emerged brilliantly like the others, and he was the oldest of the group.

Vũ Đức Gương, a Catholic and former South Vietnamese commando originally from North Vietnam, who fled to the South in 1954 after the Communists took power and who before enlisting as a commando had been a carpenter, talks about when he was saved by Martin Vik during the February 15, 1964, mission described above, although he was captured in a later mission (his fourth, always with Team NEPTUNE, on the night between March 12 and 13, 1964, and also described in summary above), also commanded by Martin. He spent sixteen years in a North Vietnamese prison along with two fellow commandos: the leader of the group, Nguyễn Văn Như (a super-tough anti-Communist who had tattooed on his chest the phrase "Kill the Communists" and received the harshest sentence: life imprisonment), and Phạm Vân Ly, while the fourth member of the team, Vũ Văn Giỏi, was killed in the encounter (these were probably the shots heard by Martin and reported in writing in Reidar Steffensen's diary). After sixteen years he did not return to the prison camp from a leave and managed to escape to America, ending up in Chicago. It was there where, interviewed shortly before 2000, Gương recognized in a photograph Martin Vik as the skipper who saved him in the described mission of February 15, 1964. Wick Tourison, in an internet forum, wrote that Gương was from Team CANCER, but Gương was actually a frogman, and only Team NEPTUNE was scuba-qualified. Furthermore, Team CANCER was made up of ethnic Nungs, while Gương was a Catholic northerner. A rotation between the team members was very unlikely, at least under CIA management.

There is widespread conviction in the community of ex-commandos that within the group, there was a double agent who informed the enemy about the time and place of the next mission: they always had the feeling of being waited for. The then ARVN captain Đỗ Văn Tiến (later lieutenant colonel), deputy chief of Project Tiger—the airborne infiltration program—but for some time in charge of the maritime operations launches from Đà Nẵng, claimed in summer 1995 on a Hanoi television station that it was he who compromised all the team launches into the North. Having said that, we must admit that the gross underestimation of North Vietnamese coastal control and surveillance capabilities accounted for just as much, if not more.

In retrospect, both Reidar and Martin have come to understand that in some parts of the crews, there were infiltrators from the Vietcong. Martin briefly commented that it is "not easy to wage war when the enemy is working on both sides."

With those premises (a classic of South Vietnamese military history, particularly of "black entry" operations in the North), it is easy to understand that almost all the raiders involved in operations ended up, sooner or later, being killed or captured. They had the feeling that they were always expected at the target by the enemy. That is possible (accounting for the logistics and service personnel who moved about these units and bases), although, in the author's opinion, the gross American underestimation of North Vietnamese abilities to monitor and keep effective watch over their coastline was another constant. The CIA declared that all the commandos who did not return presumably were dead, even when it knew of their survival in prison. That was a way to avoid paying an indemnity to the families. More than a question of stinginess, this attitude seems ascribable to an attempt to hide the creeping Americanization of the conflict until the mid-1960s. Later, the fact that it was not Americans but South Vietnamese "irregulars" meant that neither the Saigon government, for the short time that it was in existence after the Paris Accords, nor the Washington government after the war bothered much about the fate of these unfortunate commandos whom they had asked to risk their lives.

OTHER COLLATERAL EPISODES

On Christmas Eve 1963, a Norwegian merchant vessel anchored outside the harbor of Đà Nẵng to unload. Reidar believes that this was a vessel from a Stavanger shipping company, chartered by Steins Marine Line. The Vikings borrowed the small boat in which they were normally transported to the operational Swift base and headed to the merchantman themselves. The surprise among the Norwegians on board the merchant vessel was great upon seeing three fellow countrymen in Đà Nẵng. They got the telegraph operator on board to send Christmas telegrams home to Norway (this whole episode looks like a breach in security, but probably some rules were not so strictly observed nor enforced). It developed into a small party on board, and Reidar and Knut would have stayed on board and spent the night there. In the end, it was Martin who gave it a cut and wanted to go home, and the others therefore joined him in his return to Đà Nẵng.

One morning while driving from the harbor in Đà Nẵng and out to the base at work, they witnessed an accident: there had been a collision between two junks in the harbor. In the water there was a body floating. There were more than enough boats coming to rescue, so they continued to the base.

Both Reidar and Martin remember well that the Nastys came to Đà Nẵng from February onward. Yet, they had little to do with the South Vietnamese crews and the Americans who were on board these fast boats. They greeted them, of course, and exchanged a few words occasionally, but beyond this there was little contact. As stated, the Norwegians were also aware that some Germans had been hired to be on the Gassers (though they misremembered them as Nastys), but did not have much to do with these men either, although they were aware that these guys were heavy drinkers and that they were sent home.

On the way out to one of his missions, Reidar ran over a junk. The junk was split in two and destroyed. The crew of the junk ended up in the water, but Reidar turned quickly around and managed to rescue them and pick them up. Luckily all the men were unharmed, and they were taken back to the port of Đà Nẵng. When the men were safely on land, the follow-up was taken over by the Americans. Reidar then continued out to conduct the planned mission. The fishermen were given compensation in the form of a new boat, food, and other gifts.

The three Norwegians basically did not have much contact with their crews beyond the training and missions. But as the end approached and they were to return home, they arranged a farewell party for the crews.

Mostly the weather was favorable both in Đà Nẵng and during the missions. During the very first mission, however, it was awfully bad weather and a lot of wind. When they were out waiting for the dinghy, they had to sit and watch the ropes (unsure of this). The trip back was rough in the bad weather. When they entered the harbor, they went over the machinery, and then it turned out that several nuts had loosened due to the shaking and had to be tightened. But, basically, it was good weather and pretty quiet during missions, and they remember that it was only this one time they could not hold full speed. When the wind was strong while the boats were berthed, sometimes the boats had to leave the quay and be anchored out on the bay.

Martin and Reidar remember few names of the Americans and others they had anything to do with. The one they remember best is Phil Holtz. Martin later came across Phil Holtz while commanding the *Marjata*, but of course at that time Holtz was engaged in another mission. Furthermore, they say that they had a lot to do with a commander in relation to the briefs. After Phil Holtz, they had some contact with another guy. He was tall and thin, and they think his name was Hawes (*Author*: James "Jim" Hawes, from SEAL Team Two, who later joined the CIA for the Congo and other assignments). In addition, they remember a huge red-haired man, who had the nickname "Red."

As mentioned, the Americans conducted skills tests. Reidar remembers: "On a training trip we had with the Americans, we had to go far out to sea and use the sextant to take the height of the sun and calculate what position we were in. Then we got only one line of bearing, no distance, and when it got dark again, then we had to go into a place where we were going to stop. The place was purposefully chosen inside an island. It was a lot of luck that Martin did not drive up into the rocks. He had sonar on and then noticed that it started to become very shallow, and then he ordered full stop. They let out a drag and lay there until that light. The boat was right on top of the pile of rocks."

As mentioned at the beginning, all three have subsequently given some thought to what they have been involved in. A lot of thoughts have of course gone to the eight commandos whom they did not bring home. They came to know from the television documentary NRK network that some of them had gotten out of prison and made it to the United States and Canada, and that one of them (Gương) even picked out Martin in a photo. Reidar has also thought a lot about whether they also may have been involved in something illegal by being recruited in Norway. Obviously, they rethought about it all when, in the years to come, they saw from home the escalation of the Vietnam War, compared to what it was when they were hired in summer 1963.

CHAPTER
7

A Mystery
That Lingers

Rubber inflatable boat used by the South Vietnamese commandos for landing after having left the Swift boats. At the side is a 57 mm recoilless rifle sometimes used in the raids. Shown here is the boat recovered by the North Vietnamese after a failed attack on Đồng Hới on June 30, 1964, just after the Vikings had left the country. *Vietnam News Agency*

M18 57 mm recoilless rifle, sometimes used by the South Vietnamese commandos in clandestine missions. *Photo by Alf van Beem*

Swedish Carl Gustaf M45B submachine gun, one of the most popular weapons used by special and irregular forces, both South Vietnamese and American in Vietnam

RAdm. Cathal L. Flynn, US Navy. At the time of the Vikings, he was one of the Navy SEALS officers who took over maritime operations after the transfer from the CIA to the military.

As houseboats and sampans glide down the Perfume River toward Hue in Vietnam, napalm air strikes raise clouds into gray monsoon skies. This picture was taken in 1968. *AP*

South Vietnamese sea commandos in action. *From https://ngothelinh.tripod. com/biethai.html*

North Vietnamese coastal units, during training or ceremonial duty

Swift boat engine maintenance. At the time of the Norwegian skippers, maintenance and repair duties on the Swifts were performed by American personnel.

Swift boat
maintenance and
repair of propellers
and rudders

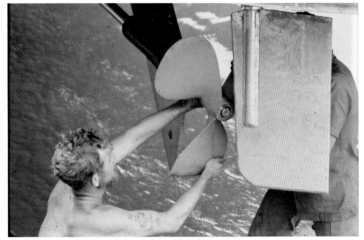

Swift boat
maintenance and
repair of propellers
and rudders

Norwegian skippers training schedule, May 11–16, 1964. *From Reidar Steffensen, via Jan Tore Nilsen*

Subj: CO qualification/refresher training schedule for LTJG THIEN and Crew 6; submission of

1. The following is the tentative schedule for subject training. Heavy operational committments will cause changes to the underway schedule. Erratas will be issued as necessary.

DATE/TIME	TRAINING	LOCATION	INSTRUCTORS
MON 3 APR	No training scheduled.		
TUES 4 APR 0900-1100	Boat familiarization, rubber dock-ing, shiphandling (1 boat)	U/W	QM, EN
1315-1515	Gunnery doctrine & safety procedures, O/B weapons familiarization.	O/B	GM
WED 5 APR 0900-1100	Practical gunnery (at sea, 1 boat)	U/W	GM, QM
1315-1500	Navigation - low visibility (radar), restricted water piloting, team vectoring, precision anchoring.	C/R	QM
THUR 6 APR 0900-1100	Engineering familiarization; light-ing off/securing, sea suction, lube oil pressure, etc.. Correction/ prevention of engineering casualties.	O/B	EN, EM
1315-1500	Shiphandling, engineering casualty drills (1 boat).	U/W	EN, EM
FRI 7 APR 0900-1100	Shiphandling, rubber docking, general drills (1 boat).	U/W	QM, EN
1315-1500	Ordnance troubleshooting & pre-ventive maintenance	O/B or Armory	GM
MON 10 APR 0900-1100	Formation tactics, anti-air, anti-surface defense, shore bombardment, maneuvering.	C/R	QM, GM
1315-1500	Tactics, firing (3 boats, beach).	U/W	QM, GM

Schedule of checkout program for the commanding-officer qualifying course (six-week program) for the South Vietnamese boat skippers. *From Reidar Steffensen, via Jan Tore Nilsen*

Swift boat in action in later years. *USN 1130649*

Swift boat helm station. Although not relevant to the Vikings period, the picture gives the basic idea of the internal spaces.

The letter of reference by the CSS for Knut Kalvenes, after his service. Dated June 15, 1964, it was signed in Saigon by Major Nguyen Binh, one of the aliases of Major Ngô Thế Linh, chief of the CSS. All three Vikings had a similar letter, with similar high praises for their performance. *Kalvenes family private collection*

HEADQUARTERS COASTAL SECURITY SERVICE
BAIGON, SOUTH VIETNAM

June 15, 1964

To Whom It May Concern:

    This is to certify that bearer:

    Mr. KNUT KALVENES, has been in the employ of this service as a Maritime Advisor from the period 15 August 1963 to date. During this period of time he has acted as the master of patrol craft and has actively participated in the training of Vietnamese crews for same.

    Subject has shown exceptional aptitude in working with the Vietnamese personnel under his command.

    He has performed extremely well under adverse circumstances with minimal supervision. Subject's contract with this service was terminated due to completion of his project in Vietnam.

    I would highly recommend him for employment in any similar work.

                                    Chief of Coastal Security Service ARVN

                                    Major NGUYEN-BINH

Swift boat PCF43 during a mission in later years

Swift boat *PCF 16* in American service

Jan Herman Linge, naval designer, and his creation, the Nasty boat, in the background. *www. ptfnasty.com*

May 11, 1960. US chief of naval operations, Adm. Arleigh Burke, with VAdm. Erling Hostvedt, Royal Norwegian Navy, disembarking from an MTB *Tjeld* (Nasty class) at Haakonsvern, south of Bergen, Norway (as noted in the original caption). Haakonsvern is the main base of the Royal Norwegian Navy and the largest naval base in the Nordic area but was officially established as RNN base only in 1962 and inaugurated by King Olav V in 1963. The author remains doubtful about the real location of this photo. *US Navy photo, NH 93680*

March 22, 1963. US president John F. Kennedy meeting with Norwegian foreign minister Halvard Lange and Norwegian defense minister Gudmund Harlem.

Gudmund Harlem, Norwegian minister of defense from 1961 to 1965, at the time of the Vikings and of the Nasty boats affair

March 22, 1963. Norwegian foreign minister Lange, *right*, and defense minister Harlem, *left*, meeting Kennedy.

March 22, 1963. Norwegian defense minister Harlem leaving at the airport, with his colleague Lange, after meeting Kennedy.

May 15, 1963, Quantico, Virginia. Secretary of the Navy Fred North aboard *PTF-3*, the first Norwegian Nasty for the US Navy. *NH94501*

May 16, 1963, Quantico, Virginia. *PTF-3*'s first XO (executive officer), Lt. j.g. Mike L. Mulford, talking to Undersecretary of the Navy Paul Fay. *NH94500*

Norwegian Nasty boat, after modifications for Vietnam (the most visible alteration is the removal of the torpedo tubes); probably off Subic Bay, Philippines. *https://ngothelinh. tripod.com/biethai. html*

Nasty boat at high speed in Vietnam. *US Navy photo*

Nasty boat helm station

Nasty boats in sea trials in 1964. *USN711288*

PTF-3 and *PTF-4* at Subic Bay, Philippines, 1964

Nasty boat on test. *US Navy photo*

Nasty-class patrol boats operated by MACV-SOG Detachment 2, return from the DMZ, 1971. *From the Frederick J. Vogel Collection (COLL/5577) at the Archives ranch, Marine Corps History Division*

Nasty boat *PTF-17. Photo by Lt Kurt Froyen, USNR, OIC PTF-19*

PTF-17 building at Trumpy and Sons, Annapolis Maryland, May 31, 1967. *PTF-17* was the first of six US-built Nasty boats, after the first fourteen were supplied directly by Norway. *Naval Photographic Center, Washington, DC; from ptfnasty.com website*

Nasty-class *PTF-6* at naval amphibious base, Little Creek, Virginia, December 1973. *PTF-6* was one of the six Nasty boats (*PTF-3* to *PTF-8*) taken directly from the stocks of the Royal Norwegian Navy, to speed up deliveries and deployment to Vietnam. *USN1157722*

Alf Martens Meyer in a late image. After retiring from active service, he settled in Spain before returning to Norway, where he died in April 1989.

Knut Kalvenes in 2000, thirty-six years later. *NRK*

An aging but smiling Knut Kalvenes

Vilhelm Evang, for a long time the chief of Norwegian military intelligence, and Meyer's superior

Jørgen Kosmo, Norway's minister of defense from 1993 to 1997, who, while in office, denied involvement or silent approval by the government of the Norwegian support at the time of the Vikings

In an interview, Vilhelm Evang, chief of Norwegian military intelligence from 1946 to 1965, said that Meyer, in directing his division, maybe went "a little too far" in cultivating his close relationship with American intelligence.

Veteran commando survivor Vũ Đức Gương, now living in Chicago, indicating Martin Vik (*in the center of the picture*) as the Norwegian skipper who saved him on the February 15, 1964, mission

Martin Øyerhavn, alias Vik, still in the gala uniform of the Royal Norwegian Navy, with his wife in 2016. *Facebook*

The whaler *Globe 14*, in 1965 bought and rebuilt as a spy ship for Norwegian military intelligence. Rebaptized *Marjata* and allegedly commanded by Martin Vik/Øyerhavn, served from 1966 to 1975 before being replaced by the *Marjata II*, of which Martin was given command.

The *Marjata II* was purpose-built as an intelligence-gathering ship by Mjellem & Karlsen shipyards, Bergen, Norway. Commissioned in 1976 and subsequently refitted, it remained in service with the Norwegian military intelligence until 1995, allegedly still commanded by Martin Vik/Øyerhavn. In 1995, it was sold to a private company, Gardline Geosurvey Ltd., and renamed *Sea Explorer*. Shown here is a night view of the ship after the sale.

The *Marjata III*. The third Norwegian spy ship to bear this name, it was commissioned in 1995 and was allegedly still, for some years, commanded by Martin.

Marjata III three-quarters view from the back

The ELINT ship FS *Marjata III* in Kirkenes, northern Norway, 8 kilometers from the Russian border

A starboard bow view of the Norwegian intelligence collection ship *Marjata III* (IMO no. 9107277) tied up at the pier in Port Everglades, Florida

Marjata III stern view

Marjata III stern view in Arctic environment

Reidar interviewed in 1993, with a map of Đà Nẵng

Reidar reading his war diary some thirty-six years after the first meeting with Alf Martens Meyer, in the same Hotel Bristol in Bergen, together with fellow skipper Knut Kalvenes. Martin, at the time still in service as naval commander with the Norwegian military intelligence, could not participate. *NRK*

A North Vietnamese Shantou-class gunboat burns near Hon Ne Island, after an attack by aircraft from the US Navy aircraft carrier USS *Constellation*, off North Vietnam's Lach Chao Estuary (Vietnamese geographical reference cửa Lạch Trường), August 5, 1964, during the Tonkin Gulf incident that triggered the American intervention in the Vietnam War.

A Swatow gunboat similar to those that the South Vietnamese commandos so often tried to sabotage in the missions described in the book. Defined by the Chinese as the Shantou class, it was known in the United States as the Swatow class. It was derived from the Soviet P-6 motor torpedo-boat class.

In today's Norway, despite a televised report by the NRK network, very little is known about this whole Viking adventure. Most likely, the Norwegian authorities still fear it could cause some embarrassment, because of this undeclared support (men and boats) to the American effort in Vietnam.

Kalvenes and Steffensen were interviewed a few times before the year 2000, while Martin Vik, longtime commander of the Norwegian ELINT/SIGINT ship *Marjata*, refused at the time to release interviews because he was still working for the Norwegian intelligence service. He still lives in a beautiful cottage on a fjord in Hatlestrand, in the same Hordaland area he came from. Knut Kalvenes, after having been engaged in the local politics in that area, passed away in early 2015, and Reidar Steffensen still lives in Fyllingsdalen, in the Hordaland area as well.

Bill Hamilton said he remembered "a dozen" Norwegians being recruited by the CIA. Only the three mentioned in this article, however, ever went to Vietnam. What about the others?

Regarding this mystery, only one hypothesis could be advanced. At that time, Bill Hamilton was responsible for all CIA MAROPS. The CIA had three clandestine naval theaters: North Vietnam, the waters around Cuba, and the Congo (operating on the Tanganyica Lake). It was by all means possible, as a logical deduction, that the other Norwegians were employed in those naval theaters outside Vietnam. But, after thorough research, the author could ascertain that the non-American sailors employed in those other two theaters were only anti-Castro Cuban nationals (according to Bill Hamilton's own written memories in his autobiography *Night Fighter*; see Hamilton and Sasser 2020). Thomas Ahern, a CIA officer who had some notoriety for being the chief of station in Tehran at the time of the 1979–81 hostage crisis, and lately for being a prominent CIA historian, but who earlier had an assignment in the Congo, stated that when he was serving there, there were no Norwegian captains on Lake Tanganyika in 1966 and that he is not aware of any having been there either before or after that year. So, we can only say that Bill Hamilton's memories were inaccurate on this detail, or that the eight Taiwanese who replaced the Norwegians were initially called the Vikings by the CIA for bureaucratic inertia, so that, summed up with the three "true" Norwegians, together they make nearly the "dozen Vikings" quoted by Hamilton, by mistake all considered as Norwegian nationals. On the other hand, RAdm. (ret.) Cathal Flynn, who at the time was directly involved in the operations, said that he knew only of the three Norwegians and that there is no way he can make up it to twelve, because he also never knew of anyone else called the Vikings. Martin, also interviewed by phone by the author, said as well that, to his knowledge, it was only the three of them, and Knut Kalvenes's son and widow confirm that to their knowledge, as well, there were only three Vikings, saying that Martin Vik/Øyerhavn was the only one who could say something more, if anything, but we see what Martin himself assumes.

Not even the Nasty boats, which were totally new craft for the US Navy and the CIA, ever saw Norwegian personnel in action or in support in Vietnam, except in a pair of cases in a later era. To assist the Americans with familiarization, Norwegian sailors of technicians from the Westermoen shipyards (the builders) were engaged, working alongside American personnel in Norfolk and San Diego, or possibly at Subic Bay in the Philippines, but certainly not in any mission in Vietnam.

The Nasty fast boats were shipped deck-loaded to America, so there was no need of an experienced Norwegian crew for that. It is possible that Norwegian commandos or combat swimmers, in a well-known US-Norway exchange and mutual-support program for underwater and special-forces activities, could have operated in conjunction with American forces, but anyway, these activities—chiefly for joint training—had nothing in common with the naval operations planned at that stage by the NAD and launched from Đà Nẵng.

James Hawes, SEAL Team Two plank owner (i.e., one of the founding members), was one of the CIA/SEAL officers responsible for the planning of the ops starting in May 1964. He is almost certain that there were no other Norwegians. In addition, Martin and Reidar cannot recall any other Norwegians in Đà Nẵng. Mike Mulford, the first XO (executive officer) on PTF 3, says they had no Norwegian mentors after they left Pearl Harbor.[1]

HOW MUCH WAS KNOWN (AND HOW MANY DID KNOW) IN OSLO?

As for the involvement of the Norwegian authorities in this story, it must be said that the Norwegian minister of defense at that time, Gudmund Harlem, made many trips to the United States for talks at the highest political and military level, also meeting President Kennedy in person.

His successor some thirty years later, Jørgen Kosmo, in office from 1993 to 1997, when interviewed about it said that Meyer must have done everything by himself in contacting the three sailors. Pressed by the journalist submitting some evidence, he finally added: "If the Americans are behind all this, they committed an illegality, but, at this point in time, I don't see what I could do about it."

Even among the three skippers, the opinions on this seem to differ. As we have seen, Reidar is convinced of a direct involvement of senior levels in the Norwegian government, let alone intelligence, in this "Norwegian connection."

Knut Kalvenes instead said that his understanding is that there was no reason for the Norwegian government to be informed. It was all very simple and informal: the Americans went to someone they knew (Meyer), asking if he could provide people with certain skills, and he just made demand and supply meet.

Concerning the structure that Meyer was part of, the E-tjenesten, Meyer was the chief of a section that had many contacts with the United States (the CIA). Vilhelm Evang, for a long time the chief of Norwegian military intelligence, and direct superior of Meyer at that time, said, "Maybe Meyer was in too-close contact with the USA, he went a little too far." The whole thing was organized so that none of the real actors (Norway-CIA-USA) could be detectable, but the general understanding is that nothing like that could have ever been done without the informed consent of senior levels of Oslo's government, though nobody knows for certain, except the CIA chief of station at the time, and the Norwegians themselves, "how high it went."

August Radtke, an old friend and colleague of Meyer, as well as his brother in arms in the Milorg, the Norwegian anti-Nazi clandestine resistance army during the war, says, as is well known, that "Meyer was the supporting pillar of the reconstitution of the postwar Norwegian intelligence service; he was a great organizer—that is, he had ideas and was able to put them into action. He was a patriot, a Norwegian intelligence patriot. All the ELINT and SIGINT radio-listening stations in the extreme north of the islands (not to mention the *Marjata*) bear his signature or his imprint. He began from the inside to extend the protection of Norwegian interests abroad as well."

The Americans had supplied all the high-tech equipment for the COMINT and SIGINT station network that the Norwegian military intelligence was setting up at the time, particularly thanks to the drive provided by Meyer, and Meyer himself could be more than willing to repay the Americans, on occasion. Three skilled sailors were not much of a big deal, after all.

The consensus is that the Norwegian intelligence knew what was actually going on, and the plan behind it. But again, on the political-level involvement, among the three Vikings themselves the feelings are not the same. Knut Kalvenes maintains that he does not believe that the Norwegian politicians were aware of it, and that the contacts occurred only between the two respective intelligence agencies.

Notes

1. "I went, in December 1962 or January 1963, to the Philadelphia Naval Shipyard and took over as first lieutenant on *PTF-3*, the first of the Norwegian NASTY Boats to come over. About a month after I got there, I took over as XO . . . just a Norwegian advisor in Virginia for a month or so, no one after that." Mike Mulford interview with Ed Marolda in 1983, Naval Historical Center; also interview in 2022 of J. Hawes and M. Mulford with Jan Tore Nilsen.

APPENDIXES

APPENDIX 1

SELECTED CHRONOLOGY FROM THE "PENTAGON PAPERS," 1963–64

From the approval in the National Security Action Memorandum No. 52 (NSAM 52) of May 11, 1963, of CIA-backed clandestine operations against NVN, to the growing number of recommendations and approvals on such activities until early 1964 to intimidate NVN. Including evaluations and assessments, not always optimistic on results to be expected.

Chronology

11 May 63. NSAM 52: Authorized CIA-sponsored covert operations against NVN.

9 Sept. 63. CINCPAC OPLAN 34-63: JCS approved this program for nonattributable "hit and run" GVN covert operations against NVN, supported by US military advisory materiel and training assistance.

1 Nov. 63. Diem overthrown: military junta led by General Minh assumed control.

20 Nov. 63. Vietnam Policy Conference, Honolulu: During high-level USG discussions of the probable consequences, political and military, of Diem's downfall, conferees agreed that military operations against the Vietcong had not been and would not be particularly upset by the changed political situation. Development of a combined MACV-CAS [*Note*: "CAS" in this text stands for "Controlled American Source," a euphemism used in Vietnam for the CIA.] program for covert operations against NVN was directed.

22 Nov. 63. President Kennedy assassinated.

26 Nov. 63. NSAM 273: authorized planning for specific covert operations, graduated in intensity, against the DRV.

19 Dec. 63. OPLAN 34A submitted by CINCPAC: the MACV-CAS plan providing a "spectrum of capabilities for the RVNAF to execute against North Vietnam" was forwarded to the JCS with CINCPAC's comment that only air attacks and a few other "punitive or attritional" operations were likely to achieve the stated objective of convincing Hanoi to cease supporting insurgents in SVN and Laos.

30 Dec. 63. Memo for the director, CIA: Assessing "Probable Reactions to Various Courses of Action with Respect to North Vietnam," the Board of National Estimates studied thirteen proposed covert operations. The BNE did not think that any would convince NVN to change its policies. Hanoi's reaction to them was forecast as mild.

2 Jan. 64. Krulak Committee Report: "Least risk" activities drawn from the 2062 in OPLAN 34A formed the basis of a twelve-month, three-phase program of covert operations. MACV would exercise operational control, and CAS and CINCPAC would train and equip the GVN, or third-nation personnel involved. Phase 1 (February–May) included intelligence collection (through U-2 and special intelligence missions), psychological operations, and some twenty "destructive" undertakings. Similar operations would be increased in number and intensity during Phases 2 and 3; destructive acts would be extended to targets "identified with North Vietnam's economic and industrial well-being." Committee members reasoned that Hanoi attached great importance to economic development, and that progressive damage to the economy—or its threatened destruction—would convince Hanoi to cancel support of insurgency. But the committee cautioned that even successful execution of the program might not induce Hanoi to "cease and desist."

1 Feb. 64. OPLAN 34A: Phase 1 of the covert activities program began.

20 Feb. 64. NSC meeting: President Johnson ordered more-rapid contingency planning for pressures—covert and overt—against North Vietnam and ordered pressures shaped to produce the maximum credible deterrent effect on Hanoi.

APPENDIX 2

THE "VIKING SHIPS": THE NASTY BOATS, SWIFT BOATS, AND THE *MARJATA* SPY SHIP

The Nasty Boats: Jan Hermann Linge, the Designer

The fast patrol boats called Nasty boats were at the time the most-advanced and highest-performance patrol torpedo boats in the world. They had been designed in the second half of the 1950s under the direction of Jan Hermann Linge, an engineer and naval designer with a past in the Norwegian anti-Nazi resistance. Jan Hermann Linge (born in Trondheim in 1922; died in Asker in 2007) was the son of Martin Jenssen Linge, who was also known for his war effort in the Kompani Linge, as we will see later.

Jan Hermann Linge went to sea when he was fifteen years old on the motor tanker *Oro* from Arendal. He thrived very well on the seven seas, and all plans for further education were put on hold. His father did not agree with his son's priorities and went out around the world to find him and bring him home. They met in Singapore, and together they boarded another ship in 1939 and made their way home.

Linge had internships at shipyards in 1940 and 1941. He started his naval-engineering studies in 1942, but the war put a temporary stop to these.

Jan Linge fled to Sweden on the self-constructed sailboat *Vito*. From there he proceeded to England with a British gunboat. Linge was trained as an SOE agent (SOE = special-operations executive, the British clandestine and sabotage operations organization meant to operate in the Nazi-occupied Europe) and was part of Kompani Linge in 1944–45. He was parachuted into the German-occupied Norway in the winter of 1944–45 as a saboteur and instructor for the Milorg (the in-country underground Norwegian army) in the D12 county (Akershus/Hedmark). Linge was later captured during an operation and sent to prison camp in Germany after Gestapo interrogation. However, he managed to escape along the way and made it over to the advancing American forces. In early April 1945, he returned to England and became an instructor for new agents.

He resumed his studies after the end of the war and studied as a naval architect in England and the United States from 1946 to 1949.

Linge worked as an engineer in A/S Westermoen Båtbyggeri and Mek Verksted shipyards in Mandal from 1949 to 1956. During this time as chief engineer, he designed the Nasty class of motor torpedo boat, which became the basis for the Tjeld class for the Royal Norwegian Navy. These boats were in production from the autumn of 1957 (the Nasty private venture prototype) until around 1970. The boats incorporated some of the best features of the American wartime PT boats and of the British Fairmile D MTBs, in close cooperation with the experience and operational needs of Norwegian wartime commanders. The crew consisted of nineteen sailors, but in Vietnam, between crewmen and commandos they were carrying up to about thirty people. A total of forty-two units of this class were built in Norway by the Westermoen shipyards of Mandel and were adopted, in addition to by the Norwegian navy (the twenty patrol boats of the Tjeld class), by the US Navy (fourteen, used in Vietnam) and in a small number by the navies of West Germany (two), Greece (six), and Turkey (the two ex-German boats used on an experimental basis by the Bundesmarine and then ceded to Turkey). In addition, six were built in the United States.

Linge later started his own boat design house, Jan H. Linge A/S, and designed many leisure boats for other companies. He was also a very active designer of sailboats. The designs by Linge are known by the "ling" suffix, such as Brisling, Firling, Fjordling, Gambling 34, Lærling, Mekling, Smiling, Wesling, and Willing. The Soling was selected as Olympic class in 1968 and participated in eight Olympic games. The Yngling became an international class in 1979, and an Olympic class in the Athens Olympics in 2004. In 1998, he was made a Knight 1st Class of the Royal Norwegian Order of St. Olav.

His father, Martin Jenssen Linge (born on December 11, 1894, on Linge Farm in Norddal, Sunnmøre, Norway; died on December 27, 1941, in Måløy, on South Vågsøy in Sogn og Fjordane, Norway), was killed in action on December 27, 1941, during Operation Archery at the Lofoten islands, leading the Norwegian volunteer company trained by the British SOE, the Norwegian Independent Company 1, in short NOR.I.C1 (pronounced as *Norisén* in Norwegian).

Shortly after the German attack on Norway on April 9, 1940, he traveled to Åndalsnes to join his regiment. He had previously attained the rank of lieutenant (in the reserve forces) and was also one of the first Norwegians to obtain a pilot's license. When British troops landed at Åndalsnes on April 17, Linge became liaison officer between the local regiment and the British. Åndalsnes (and other towns in Møre og Romsdal County) was at this time still unoccupied territory, and the only port with railway connections to eastern Norway and the campaign there. The king, the crown prince, the cabinet, Norway's gold and cash holdings, and finally Major General Otto Ruge, with staff, escaped through Åndalsnes. Trygve Lie, in his memoirs, recalls meeting Linge at Åndalsnes. During German air bombing of a makeshift airfield at Setnesmoen, he was wounded and evacuated by boat to Britain. He was the first wounded Norwegian soldier to arrive in Britain.

Among exiled Norwegians, Martin Linge along with Nordahl Grieg and Olav Rytter were the first to propose ideas for resistance against the German occupation. "Our land is perfect for secret resistance and guerrilla warfare," he declared in June 1940. In August 1940, he was appointed as liaison officer to the War Office and soon began recruiting men and organizing what became Norwegian Independent Company 1.

Martin Jenssen Linge was killed during Operation Archery, a British Combined Operations raid at Måløy against German military positions on Vågsøy Island. During the occupation of Norway by Nazi Germany, Måløy was used as a German coastal fortress, which had led to the eradication of all settlements on the island to make room for the fortress. His body is buried at the Vestre gravlund (Western Cemetery) in Oslo.

Subsequently, the unit he had led was rebaptized Kompani Linge in his honor. Linge Company was more formally known as Lingekompaniet (the Linge Company).

The Nasty Boats, Technical Details

The Nasty boats, which were born as patrol boats, had a special laminated mahogany hull and displaced about 75 tons at full load. They had a 24.7-foot beam with a draft (immersion) of 3.7 feet at the bow and 6.1 feet at the stern. Cargo capacity was up to 18 tons, or 6,100 US gallons of fuel, which at cruising speed resulted in a range of 1,000 nautical miles. The Nastys were powered by two British eighteen-cylinder Napier Deltic turbo-charged diesel engines, which together developed 6,200 hp (4,623 kW), allowing a maximum speed of 35 knots at full load, and could accelerate to nearly 50 knots in emergency, although with "normal load" (DWL design waterline load).

Armament included a bow-mounted 40 mm Bofors gun (later replaced by an 81 mm mortar and a .50-caliber machine gun), while a second 40 mm Bofors gun was mounted aft, with a 20 mm Rheinmetall cannon on each side of the gangway. The four original 533 mm torpedo tubes were removed by the Americans for use in Vietnam, transforming the craft into fast patrol boats or gunboats. Equipment and navigation aids included, among other things, a depth recorder and a Decca radar with a 50-nautical-mile range. The main radar screen was located in the Combat Information Center (CIC), with various monitors and repeaters situated on the bridge. The radar was used mainly for operations or for navigation, but the antenna could be made to swing up by 15 degrees if necessary to act as an air defense radar. The radar was modern, but the electronic circuitry of the era used LEDs, which broke down easily in rough seas. Radio communications were telephonic or in code.

One peculiar characteristic of the Nasty boats was the ability to directly and easily control the engines during tactical operations or in an emergency, without having to give orders to the engine officer. The bridge was not covered, did not have seats, and was relatively low, so as to present as little surface as possible to side winds. Pitch was pronounced at high speeds. On the bridge, one had to be prepared "in position" to anticipate and get along with the ship's movements and to avoid being soaked by spray and waves. The laminated wood hull of the Nasty was robust and suited to deal with rough sea conditions without damage. The Nasty PT boats were very much liked by their captains and became the backbone of the Sea Patrol Force. The clear comment by Bill Hamilton, then in charge of CIA naval operations, was "They were damn fine boats!" Ironically, as we have seen, the Norwegian boats were never commanded in Vietnam by Norwegian captains.

The first two Nasty PT boats acquired by the Americans were handed over to the US Navy in 1963 at Little Creek, Virginia, where, following a series of tests, they were baptized *PTF-3* and *PTF-4*. On May 3, 1963, the two boats were transferred to San Diego, California, for personnel training. On September 17, they were loaded aboard USS *Defiance* (landing ship dock, LSD-31) as far as Pearl Harbor, and from there to Subic Bay in the Philippines a month later. At Subic Bay, supplementary fuel tanks were installed; to get the necessary space, the forward 40 mm gun and its ammunition storage area were removed. The 40 mm gun was replaced by an 81 mm mortar and .50-caliber machine gun.

Thomas J. Highstreet, in *RiverAce . . . Cold Warrior* (Highstreet 2004), at the time just detached from the Navy to the Army, which wanted him for duty in Vietnam, recalls his sensation and experience in Subic Bay after the work was completed and the Nastys were outfitted and ready for sailing: "It was an amazing craft," . . . "This was going to be fun! . . . We were out every day in Manila Bay . . . even at maximum, the throttles could be pushed to reverse in one smooth motion, and the boat would immediately respond." To finish with "the final, classy touch . . . each member of the crew received a coffee mug with a Norwegian crest on one side, and our name in gold on the other side. How thorough those people [the Norwegians] were in creating a vessel worthy of warfare."

Mike Mulford, for his part, says this about the Nastys: "The engines were British-built Napier Deltic. Very good engines. They had a tendency to blow liners, but they developed, as I remember it, 3,120 horsepower each. There were two engines in a boat. A very compact, a very, very good boat. Tremendously good acceleration. You could go flying along at 45 knots at max, grab the throttles, ram them into reverse; they had an automatic clutching mechanism that would slow the boat down, stop it, and start backing it up. And you could stop it on one or two boat lengths. Of course, it threw anybody on deck flat on their face. But very good boats . . . highly maneuverable." The Norwegian boats were very reliable boats.

On February 22, 1964, both boats were loaded aboard USS *Carter Hall* to be transported to Vietnam. While being hauled aboard, PTF-3 suffered serious damage that forced it to be returned to Subic Bay for repairs. PTF-3 later reached Đà Nẵng in late February 1964. The first CO was Lt. j.g. John Graham, and the XO was Lt. j.g. Michael J. Mulford, who recently (2020) confirmed that there were no Norwegians involved in the training and maintenance of the Nastys after delivery to the US.

On February 1, 1964, Norway ceded another four Nasty boats to the Americans in Bergen. Baptized respectively as *PTF-5, PTF-6, PTF-7*, and *PTF-8*, they were loaded aboard USS *Point Barrow* (AKD-1) to be transported to Subic Bay in the Philippines by March 3. A few months later, following refitting and various upgrades, these craft also reached Vietnam.

No matter what the original intentions were, by the time the Norwegian-made Nasty boats arrived in Vietnam and became operational, the clandestine maritime operations had already been handed over to the military. MACV-SOG was established in Saigon on January 24, 1964, and officially on February 1. Navy lieutenant Burton Knight was the new chief in Đà Nẵng of a new US unit, Naval Advisory Detachment (NAD), from the US Navy Pacific Command (CINPAC). However, some CIA officers, due to their irreplaceable experience, kept managing and supporting those activities until 1965, although with a progressively diminishing role. So, my understanding is that the CIA, as a matter of fact, never directly managed the Norwegian Nasty boats once they were operational "in country," in Vietnam.

The Swifts

The three Swift boats on which the Norwegians operated were quite a bit smaller. Built by the Sewart Seacraft shipyards of Berwick, Louisiana, which produced 193 examples in three versions, they were derived from craft that serviced offshore oil platforms.

They had an aluminum hull and a length of 15 meters, displaced 19 tons, and had a draft of little more than 1 meter, which made them suitable for employment in coastal waters and in the rivers of Vietnam. They were powered by two General Motors 12V71 Detroit Marine Diesel engines, which pushed them at 28 knots. Standard armament was a .50-caliber twin mount and an 81 mm mortar with another .50-caliber machine gun. Crew consisted, in theory, of five men. In action with the Norwegians, they generally transported a four-man commando or frogman squad.

From the time the control of the missions passed to MACV-SOG, the boats were placed under command of the Mobile Support Team (MST), which at the time (March 1964) was commanded by the above-mentioned Lt. Burton Lee Knight, who was thus the direct superior of the three Vikings, of whom he had a high opinion (as stated in an interview with Knight by Prof. Moise in 1989). Knight died on February 27, 1995, in Columbia, Maryland.

The Swift boat was conceived in a staff study by the Naval Advisory Group, Military Assistance Command, Vietnam (NAVADGRP MACV), titled *Naval Craft Requirements in a Counter Insurgency Environment*, published February 1, 1965. It noted that "counterinsurgency water operations are difficult, demanding, and unique. A prevalent belief has been that COIN craft can readily be obtained from existing commercial and naval sources when needed. Unfortunately, no concerted effort has been made to develop COIN craft specifically suited to perform the many missions needed to combat insurgent activities."

The study went on to list the desirable specifications of the ideal patrol craft:

reliable and sturdy

nonwooden hull, with screw and rudder protection against groundings

self-sufficient for 400-to-500-mile (600–800 km) patrol

speed of 20 to 25 knots (37–46 km/h)

small high-resolution radar range 4 to 6 miles (7–11 km)

reliable long-range communications equipment, compatible with Army
   and Air Force

quiet

armament for limited offense

sparse berthing, no messing

depth meter accurate from 0 to 50 feet (15 m)

small, powerful searchlight

The study was positively received, and the Navy began to search for sources. Sewart Seacraft of Berwick, Louisiana, built water taxis for companies operating oil rigs in the Gulf of Mexico, which appeared nearly ideal. The Navy bought their plans and asked Sewart Seacraft to prepare modified drawings that included a gun tub, ammo lockers, bunks, and a small galley. The Navy used those enhanced plans to request bids from other boat builders, but Sewart Seacraft was eventually chosen to build the boats.

The Swift boats had welded aluminum hulls about 50 feet (15 m) long, with a 13-foot (4.0 m) beam and draft of about 5 feet (1.5 m). They were originally powered by a pair of General Motors 12V71"N" Detroit Marine Diesel engines, rated at 480 horsepower (360 kW) each, with a design range from 320 nautical miles (590 km) at 21 knots (39 km/h) to about 750 nautical miles (1,390 km) at 10 knots (19 km/h). However, the Swifts used in Vietnam by the Vikings had some modifications, including more-powerful engines that allowed the boats to reach 28 knots. We have seen that the Norwegians had three South Vietnamese crewmen with them on board. In contrast, the normal complement for a Swift boat like those deployed officially from 1965 onward was six: an officer in charge (skipper), a boatswain's mate (enlisted member who is rated or "striking" for the rating as a deck seaman; the colloquial form of address for a boatswain's mate is "Boats"), a radar/radioman (radarman), an engineer (engineman), and two gunners (quartermaster and gunner's mate). In 1969, the crew was supplemented with a Vietnamese trainee.

The original water taxi design had been enhanced with two .50-caliber M2 Browning machine guns in a turret above the pilothouse, an over-and-under .50-caliber machine gun, an 81 mm mortar combination mounted on the rear deck, a mortar ammunition box on the stern, and improved habitability equipment such as bunks, a refrigerator and freezer, and a sink. The 81 mm combination mortar mounted on the rear deck was not a gravity-firing mortar as used by the Army and Marine Corps, in which the falling projectile's primer struck the fixed firing pin at the base of the mortar tube, but a unique lanyard firing weapon in which the projectile was still loaded into the muzzle. The gunner could "fire at will" by the use of the lanyard. The weapon had been tested in the 1950s and discarded as the US Navy lost interest in the system. The United States Coast Guard maintained the gun/mortar system before the Navy incorporated it into the PCF program. Many boats also mounted a single M60 machine gun in the forward peak tank, just in front of the forward superstructure.

The original order for fifty boats was followed shortly by an additional order for fifty-four more Mark Is. It is commonly believed that the heavy armament and additional installed equipment did not help the speed and seaworthiness of the somewhat underpowered Swifts.

In the second half of 1967, forty-six Mark II boats were manufactured, with a modified deckhouse set farther back from the bow. The newer boats also had round portholes (replacing the previous larger sliding windows) in the aft superstructure. From 1969 through 1972, thirty-three Mark IIIs, which were a larger version of the Mark IIs, arrived in Vietnam.

Most of the 193 PCFs built were used by the US Navy in Vietnam and the two training bases in California. About eighty were eventually sold or given away to nations friendly to the United States. The original training base for Swift boats was at Naval Amphibious Base Coronado. In 1969, training was moved to Mare Island, near San Pablo Bay, California, where it remained for the duration of the war. Though not a deepwater boat, PCF training boats frequently transited from Mare Island under the Golden Gate Bridge, to cruise either north or south along the Pacific Ocean coastline.

Vietnam Service

It is often reported that the first two PCFs were delivered to the Navy in late August 1965. We know that this is inaccurate: the Norwegians operated on three Swifts from the late summer of 1963. The year 1965 is when the US Navy selected and officially deployed the Swift boats for brown-water operations in Vietnam, functioning as the CIA MAROPS strictly covert and nonattributable operations, at least in theory.

The boats of this "official" wave were initially used as coastal patrol craft in Operation Market Time, interdicting seaborne supplies on their way to the Vietcong and PAVN forces in South Vietnam. However, the design's shallow draft and low freeboard limited its seaworthiness in open waters. These limitations, plus the difficulties being encountered in the interior waterways by the smaller, more lightly armed PBRs, led to the incorporation of Swifts to patrol the 1,500 miles (2,400 km) of rivers and canals of Vietnam's interior waterways. Swift boats continued to operate along the Vietnamese coastal areas, but with the start of Adm. Zumwalt's "SEALORDS" riverway interdiction strategy, their primary area of operations soon centered on the Cà Mau Peninsula and the Mekong delta area in the southern tip of Vietnam. Here they patrolled the waterways and performed special operations, including gunfire support, troop and Navy SEAL teams' insertion and evacuation, and raids into enemy territory.

The Mekong delta is composed of 10,000 square miles of marshland, swamps, and forested areas. The region is interlaced by rivers and canal ways. Controlled by the Vietcong, the interior waterways of the Mekong delta were used to transport supplies and weapons.

Four of these boats were lost between 1966 and 1969, but several others that had been lost to river mines or other reasons had been salvaged and either repaired or "cannibalized" for spare parts.

What the US Navy Called PTF Boats in Vietnam

The two WWII-era-designed, US-built, 1950s vintage, legacy boats (the unreliable "Gassers"), named *PTF-1* (ex-*PT-810*) and *PTF-2* (ex-*PT-811*), were pulled out of mothballs and sent to Vietnam, in the absence of anything better at hand. They were nicknamed "Gassers" because they burned gasoline or, better, aviation gasoline, rather than diesel fuel:

PT-810: Laid down December 1, 1948, by Bath Iron Works, Bath, Maine. Launched June 2, 1950. Completed November 24, 1951. Struck from the Naval Register on November 1, 1959. Reinstated on the Naval Register and reclassified as a fast patrol craft, *PTF-1*, December 21, 1962. Sunk as a target on August 1, 1965, off Vietnam.

PT-811: Laid down March 17, 1949, by John Trumpy and Sons, Annapolis, Maryland. Launched November 30, 1950. Completed March 6, 1951. Struck from the Naval Register on November 1, 1959. Reinstated on the Naval Register and reclassified as a fast patrol craft, *PTF-2*, on December 21, 1962. Sunk as a target in August 1965, off the Hawaiian Islands.

The first six Norwegian-built Nasty-class boats were taken directly from the Royal Norwegian Navy stocks and sold to the US (named *PTF-3* to *PTF-8*).

Another eight Norwegian-built Nastys were purchased and built on purpose for the US by the Norwegian Westermoen shipyards (*PTF-9* to *PTF-16*). In total, fourteen "made in Norway" Nasty boats were delivered from 1962 through 1966.

The six US-built Nasty boats of the same Norwegian design and components were assembled by John Trumpy & Sons in Annapolis, Maryland. Between Norway and the US, a grand total of twenty Nasty boats were manufactured (the American Osprey-type fast boats arrived later and won't be covered here).

In early 1964, a total of eight PTFs arrived in three increments: PTFs 1–4 (including the US "Gassers" *PTF-1* and *PTF-2*), 5–6, and 7–8.

The initial overall control over PT operations in Vietnam was under Edward Lansdale, the high-ranking CIA official who in the 1950s had established the Stay Behind network in Vietnam. But, as we know, operational control of the PTFs in Vietnam was exercised by the MACV-SOG since January 24, 1964, and the first Nasty boats arrived in Vietnam not earlier than the end of February.

Marjata, the Norwegian Spy Ship, Last Command of Martin Vik/Øyerhavn

The name *Marjata* itself reflects the personal management style of Alf Martens Meyer. The name simply is composed of the initials of his next of kin. The "M" stands for his own nickname ("Mamen"), and the "A" for his wife, Annie Signe, followed by their sons, Roy, Jan, and Alf, and their daughters-in-law, Turid and Anne Lis.

The current (2022) ship is the fourth bearing the name *Marjata*. The first was operative in the 1966–1975 period, the second in the 1976–1995 period, and the third from 1995, still operating but renamed FS *Eger*, the "ugly duckling."

The first ship, on which Martin took command, was a former whaler named *Globe 14*. In 1965, the Norwegian intelligence service cast its eyes upon a large whaling ship that was more than 51 meters long and 613 gross tons and was still in circulation. The Norwegian armed forces acquired it for 300,000 crowns at that time. It was rebuilt as a spy ship by a Bergen shipyard. Among other things, the original steam engine was replaced by a new diesel engine. Rebaptized *Marjata*, it was registered as property of the Armed Forces Research Institute. Officially, the *Marjata* was an oceanographic research vessel, but in reality it was a spy ship. On board was a large operations room with space for five operators who monitored radar, radio apparatus, and search-and-location gear. Personnel who could speak and understand Russian listened in on Soviet radio communications. The summer was "intelligence season." In winter, the *Marjata* was anchored at Kirkenes, while its personnel served in the listening station at Finnmark.

The ex-whaler was in intelligence service until 1975, when it was replaced by a new *Marjata*, purpose-built for the mission. The former whaler continued to serve in the navy after being rebuilt as a patrol vessel in the mid-1970s, now as a patrol vessel in the Varangerfjord, the most northeasterly fjord in Norway, on the Barents Sea, with the name KNM *Vadsø* (KNM for Kongelige Norske Marine), and pennant number P340, until it was sold to private parties in 1985. The third *Marjata*, with a decidedly unusual look to it, with an almost triangular plan, was also customized for advanced operations.

It entered service in 1995 and is still in service, along with the new (and for now the latest) *Marjata*, changing its name to *Eger*. Among other things, the third *Marjata* was in the area when the Russian submarine

Kursk was lost in August 2000. During the salvage operations that followed, the Norwegians cooperated with the Russians to the point that several Russian officers were allowed on board the *Marjata*.

The fourth and latest *Marjata* entered service in 2016 and is by far the largest of the series. The ship is 5,000 gross tons and measures 126 meters long and 23.5 meters wide.

BIOGRAPHICAL NOTES: AMERICANS, NORWEGIANS, AND VIETNAMESE

Châu Heng Xương: Ethnic Nung Team CANCER operator. Captured during the mission of March 16, 1964.

Colby, William Egon (born April 4, 1920, Saint Paul, Minnesota; died April 27, 1996, Rock Point, Maryland): Chief of CIA's Far East Division; later became director of the CIA between 1973 and 1976

Đỗ Văn Tiến: Captain; traitor who leaked the info on missions to the North

Elliott, David: US Army sergeant, linguist, and interpreter, present on Paradise Island in the mission of May 27, 1964

Evang, Vilhelm Andreas Wexelsen (born November 9, 1909, Aker, Norway; died January 5, 1983, Oslo, Norway): Head of the Norwegian intelligence service, 1946–66, direct superior of Alf Martens Meyer

Flynn, Cathal "Irish" Liam: Rear admiral (born July 15, 1938, Dublin, Ireland; died February 25, 2021, Coronado, California). Commissioned as an ensign, USNR, in June 1960 and then completed the UDT Replacement Training Course in Little Creek, Virginia. Flynn's first assignments are as follows: platoon officer, UDT 11 and SEAL Team One; SEAL Detachment commander with Special Operations Group, Đà Nẵng, Vietnam, 1964.

Gougelmann, Tucker Pierre Edward Power (born January 24, 1917; died June 23, 1975?): US Marine in World War II, legend in the CIA. He was responsible for clandestine maritime operations in Đà Nẵng at the time of the Vikings.

Graham, John: Navy lieutenant junior grade, the first commanding officer of *PTF-3*

Hamilton, William H., Jr. (born 1927, San Diego, California; died 2016, Virginia Beach, Virginia): Navy captain and CIA officer. Served as a fighter pilot in the Korean War. In 1961, he became the commander of UDT-21, in Little Creek, Virginia, where, with Roy Boehm as his operations officer, he was involved in developing the Navy SEAL program. Hamilton subsequently conducted missions with SEALs and the CIA in Cuba, Vietnam, Latin America, and Africa. In 1963, he was the CIA officer responsible for clandestine MAROPS, a place that he held for several years before rejoining the Navy. Hamilton retired from the Navy as a captain in 1986.

Hawes, James "Jim" M.: Navy lieutenant. As a US Navy SEAL (Class 29, attached to SEAL Team Two), he served with Navy SEAL Team Two in Vietnam and later as a CIA contractor in the Congolese Operation. The first SEAL Teams (#1 West Coast and #2 East Coast) were commissioned in 1962. Jim's batch Class #29 graduated in 1963, with him as an ensign. Upon graduation, Jim became a UDT instructor before being deployed to SEAL Team Two. He subsequently volunteered for duty in Vietnam and became one of the first SEAL officers permanently assigned there as part of CIA's OpPlan 34-A, governing covert operations into North Vietnam. He was part of the SEALS Detachment that replaced the former one in service the previous year, and he's one of those whom the Norwegians remember better after all these years. Jim served with SEAL Team Two in Vietnam from spring 1964 into 1965. Then the CIA tapped Hawes to deploy to the Congo, sometime in 1965, where he would be tasked with creating and leading a paramilitary mercenary navy (anti-Castro Cuban sailors) on Lake Tanganyika to disrupt guerrilla action in the country in 1965–66.

Highstreet, Thomas J.: Army and Navy officer, Nasty boat skipper

Holtz, Phil (sometimes referred to as "Holts"): Navy lieutenant junior grade from SEAL Team One, then CIA officer. Main assistant of Gougelmann in Đà Nẵng for MAROPS planning, and in close contact with the Norwegians. By 1963 he was already in the CIA, where he made a career and later became chief of station in San José de Costa Rica, at the time of the Iran-Contra affair. As Wick Tourison said, "He's been around for a long time." Only very recently, he agreed to talk about this story, being contacted by Jan Tore Nilsen.

Kalvenes, Knut (born September 14, 1936, Austevoll, Hordaland, Norway; died January 5, 2015, Storebø, Austevoll, Hordaland, Norway): Viking, later businessman, exponent of the Norwegian Conservative Party, and mayor of the municipality of Austevoll from 1982 to 1985

Knight, Burton Lee (born June 25, 1927, in Mount Holly, New Jersey; died February 27, 1995, at Walter Reed Army Medical Center, Bethesda, Maryland): Lieutenant commander. When MACV-SOG was established on January 24, 1964, Knight was the new chief of the Mobile Support Team One (MST-1) in Đà Nẵng, becoming the direct superior of the Norwegians.

Layton, Gilbert Baird "Chink" (born February 19, 1911, Washington, DC; died May 2, 1996, Fairfax, Virginia): Army colonel and CIA officer. During World War II, he served in the Third Army in Europe. Joined the CIA in 1950. Layton served in Vietnam from 1960 to 1964, as chief of the so-called CIA Combined Studies Group (CSG), where he directed intelligence and special operations activities, keeping the cover title of Army colonel.

Linge, Jan Hermann (born 1922, Trondheim, Norway; died 2007, Asker, Norway): The naval designer of the Nasty boats

Linge, Martin Jenssen (born December 11, 1894, Norddal, Norway; died December 27, 1941, Måløy, Norway): Jan Hermann's father

McCormack, Dennis K. (born December 31, 1938, Brooklyn, New York; died May 1, 2020): US Navy SEAL Team One plank owner, detached to SEAL Team Two, and in this assignment deployed to Vietnam in early 1964, as one of the main instructors of the South Vietnamese frogmen and commandos

Meyer, Alf "Mamen" Martens (born July 15, 1908, Bergen, Norway; died April 1, 1989, Bærum, near Oslo, Norway): Norwegian spymaster. High-ranking intelligence officer, recruiter of the three Vikings for the CIA. Already active in the Milorg, the underground army in the German-occupied Norway, during World War II. Architect of the rebirth and development of the postwar Norwegian military intelligence.

Mulford, Mike L.: Navy captain, first XO of *PTF-3* Nasty boat.

Ngô Thế Linh (a.k.a. "Major Nguyen Binh" and "Colonel Binh," as secret operative names) (born December 6, 1928, Hà Tĩnh Province, Vietnam, French Indochina; died February 25, 1999, San Jose, California): Major, commander of the Coastal Security Service. After the fall of South Vietnam, he fled to the United States.

Nguyễn Văn Như: Team leader of Team NEPTUNE, combat swimmer, UDT scuba diver. Captured during the mission between March 16 and 17, after a manhunt that lasted some days. Sentenced to life inprisonment.

Nguyễn Văn Sắc: South Vietnamese raider, captured in the mission on the night of 15 March 1964. Tried by the North Vietnamese, sentenced to death and shot, due also to his past service with the French colonial army.

Phạm Vân Ly: Team NEPTUNE operator, combat swimmer, UDT scuba diver. Captured during the mission between March 16 and 17.

Raymond, Donald C.: Navy SEALS HM1 (hospital corpsman first class, an enlisted medical specialist), "Don" and "Doc" as nicknames. Among the first wave of SEAL Team One to arrive in Vietnam to train and assist the Vietnamese commandos in maritime infiltrations from Đà Nẵng.

Russell, Clyde R. (born August 29, 1914, Nebraska; died November 3, 1979, Fayetteville, North Carolina): Colonel; World War II and Korean War veteran; in 1963, as one of the first US Army advisors with Military Assistance Command Vietnam, Russell set in motion the scenario that led to the 1964 Gulf of Tonkin incident, which led to America's full involvement in the Vietnam War. Russell was asked, in 1964, by the White House and the Joint Chiefs of Staff at the Pentagon to create a "Top Secret special operations group" to spearhead the war effort in Southeast Asia. He created and was the first commander of what eventually came to be known as MACV-SOG. Russell called his newly created unit "the Studies and Observations Group" (SOG) to keep it more arcane sounding. Of this unit, the NAD (Naval Advisory Detachment) was the maritime operations branch, reporting to the US Navy Pacific Command (CINPAC). Following Vietnam, Russell was nominated for the brigadier general's list but was then removed because of his age.

Steffensen, Reidar (born 1938): Viking; after Vietnam he lived a normal working life.

Sullivan, Robert F. (born March 26, 1931; died April 25, 2019): Navy SEALS CPO (chief petty officer), "Chief Sullivan," nicknamed "Mr. Bob" in his first Vietnam assignment and "Sully" in his second. Among the first wave of SEAL Team One to arrive in Vietnam to train and assist the Vietnamese commandos in maritime infiltrations from Đà Nẵng.

Thomas, Albert: Navy commander, chief of the NAD in 1964

Trương Duy Tài: Captain, commander of the Sea Commandos

Trương Văn Lê: Ethnic Nung Team CANCER operator. Captured in a mission in the night between March 16 and 17, 1964.

Vik (Øyerhavn), Martin (born 1935): Viking; "the chief," simply because he was the elder of the three. The only one to see active service again, after repatriation, in the military intelligence, as commander of the spy ship *Marjata*.

Voong A Cầu: Ethnic Nung Team CANCER operator. Captured by the North Vietnamese during the mission of 16 March, 1964, after a four-day manhunt, and evaded from prison fourteen years later.

Vũ Đức Gương (or Gương Đức Vũ): Team NEPTUNE operator, combat swimmer, UDT scuba diver. Captured during the mission between March 16 and 17, after a manhunt. After sixteen years in prison, he got a short leave, managed to flee to Thailand and then to the United States.

Vũ Văn Giỏi: Team NEPTUNE operator, combat swimmer, UDT scuba diver. Killed in action on the night between March 12 and 13, 1964.

BIBLIOGRAPHY AND SOURCES

Books

Ahern, Thomas L. *The Way We Do Things: Black Entry Operations into North Vietnam, 1961–1964*. Washington DC: Center for the Study of Intelligence, Central Intelligence Agency, 2005.

Aspøy, Arild. "Norges Hemmelige Vietnam krig—Vi menn." Article, June 15, 1993.

Chomsky, Norm, and Howard Zinn. *The Pentagon Papers*. 5 vols. Senator Gravel edition. Boston: Beacon, 1971.

Colby, William E. *Honorable Men: My Life in the CIA*. New York: Simon & Schuster, 1978.

Conboy, Kenneth, and Dale Andradé. *Spies and Commandos: How America Lost the Secret War in North Vietnam*. Lawrence: University Press of Kansas, 2000.

Giorgi, Alessandro. *Cronaca della Guerra del Vietnam, 1961–1975*. Florence: Luca Poggiali Editore, Vicchio, 2016.

Giorgi, Alessandro. "Vichinghi in Vietnam" (2 parts). *Storia & Battaglie* monthly magazine, October/November 2012 issues, Editoriale Lupo, Florence.

Hamilton, William H., Jr., and Charles W. Sasser. *Night Fighter: An Insider's Story of Special Ops from Korea to Seal Team 6*. New York: Arcade, 2020.

Highstreet, Thomas J. *RiverAce . . . Cold Warrior*. Indianapolis, IN: Authorhouse, 2004.

JCS–MACV-SOG Documentation Study (Draft). Maritime Operations, 10 July 1970 (FOIA declassified).

Manning, Robert, and Samuel Lipsman, eds. *War in the Shadows: Covert Operations in Vietnam*. The Vietnam Experience 25. Boston: Boston Publishing, 1988.

Marolda, Edward J., and Oscar P. Fitzgerald. *The United States Navy and the Vietnam Conflict: From Military Assistance to Combat, 1959–1965*. Washington, DC: US Government Printing Office, 1986.

Moïse, Edwin E. *Tonkin Gulf and the Escalation of the Vietnam War*. Chapel Hill: University of North Carolina Press, 1996.

Prados, John. *Presidents' Secret Wars: CIA and Pentagon Covert Operations since World War II*. New York: William Morrow, 1986.

Shultz, Richard H., Jr. *The Secret War against Hanoi*. New York: HarperCollins, 2000.

Tourison, Sedgwick D., Jr. *Secret Army, Secret War: Washington's Tragic Spy Operations in North Vietnam*. Annapolis, MD: US Naval Institute Press, 1995.

Tran Do Can. "The Gulf Raiders." In *Florida Vie Bao Directory Yearbook 2000*. Miramar, FL: Chu Ba Yen, 2000.

Interviews

Telephone conversation and email exchange with Sedgwick Tourison in 2012.

Telephone conversation with Ping Tourison.

Telephone conversation and email exchange with Svanhild Caroline Kalvenes and Svein Arne Kalvenes (widow and son of Knut Kalvenes, respectively).

Telephone conversation with Trude Steffensen (Reidar Steffensen's daughter.).

Telephone conversation with Capt. (ret.) William "Bill" Henry Hamilton in 2016.

Email exchange with Thomas Ahern in 2016.

Telephone conversation with RAdm. (ret.) Cathal L. Flynn in 2017.

Telephone conversation with Martin Øyerhavn in 2017.

Telephone conversation and email exchange with two former CIA agents whom I won't name.

Email exchange with Hung Ngo (son of Ngô Thế Linh).

Telephone conversations and extensive email exchange with Jan Tore Nilsen in 2020 and 2022.

Interview of Reidar Steffensen for *Maritimt Magasin* in 2009.

Interview with Capt. William H. Hamilton, USN, interview conducted by Edward J. Marolda, February 28, 1984. Naval Historical Center, Washington, DC.

Documentary

Aspøy Arild, dir. *Vi som støtter Amerika: Norges rolle i Vietnamkrigen* ("We who support America: Norway's role in the Vietnam War"). Television documentary by the Norwegian network NRK, broadcast in 2000. Research in the United States by Sedgwick Tourison.

Websites

www.ngothelinh.tripod.com.
https://cnsalutes.wordpress.com/tag/seal-team-one/.
https://sealtwo.org/seal-team-two/.

ACKNOWLEDGMENTS

I am particularly grateful to Cecilie Grina Iversen, assistant to the military attaché at the Norwegian embassy in Rome, for her kind and supportive availability in translating for me "on the spot" the interviews given by the Vikings; to NRK and particularly to Janne Haanes; to Jan Tore Nilsen, former Royal Norwegian naval officer, a passionate researcher who helped me clarify several details of the story, interviewing again Martin and Reidar, among others; to Wick Tourison (RIP) for his invaluable help and the great courtesy in discussing with me some details of the story, before passing away; to Professor Edwin Moïse of Clemson University for his help and availability; to Brian Sullivan (former professor at Yale and Naval War College in Newport, and Marine artillery officer in Vietnam); to Hung Ngo, son of Colonel Ngô Thế Linh, legend of the South Vietnamese Special Forces; to Martin Øyerhavn; to Svanhild Caroline Kalvenes and Svein Arne Kalvenes (widow and son of Knut Kalvenes, respectively); to Thomas Ahern; to RAdm. (ret.) Cathal L. Flynn (RIP); to Capt. (ret.) William "Bill" Henry Hamilton (RIP); to Erasmo "Doc" Riojas, veteran of SEAL Team Two, a precious source of information; to Ralph Riccio, the invaluable and patient translator of my Italian and "scrambled English" drafts (besides former US Army officer and prolific military history author), and last but not least, to my colleague and friend Van Huyen Truong.

I will never thank all the people at Schiffer Publishing enough: particularly John Stone, the acquisitions editor without whom this project would simply not have started, Bob Biondi (my outstanding developmental editor), Ginny Strauser, Carey Massimini, and of course Pete Schiffer.

INDEX